16 · January 2018

COOKBOOK

WW Flex
COOKBOOK

THE SMALL PRINT

EGGS We use medium eggs, unless otherwise stated. Pregnant women, the elderly and children should avoid recipes with eggs which are raw or not fully cooked.

FRUIT AND VEGETABLES

Recipes use medium-size fruit and veg, unless otherwise stated.

REDUCED-FAT SOFT CHEESE

Where a recipe uses reduced-fat soft cheese, we mean a soft cheese with 30% less fat than its full-fat equivalent.

LOW-FAT SPREAD

When a recipe uses a low-fat spread, we mean a spread with a fat content of no more than 39%. Microwaves If we have used a microwave in any of our recipes, the timings will be for an 850-watt microwave oven.

PREP AND COOK TIMES

These are approximate and meant to be guidelines only. The prep time includes all the steps up to and following the main cooking time(s). The stated cook times may vary according to your oven.

GLUTEN FREE Recipes labelled as gluten free, or displaying the gluten free icon, only include ingredients that naturally do not contain gluten. Whenever using tinned, bottled or other types of packaged processed ingredients, such as sauces and stocks, it is essential to check that those ingredients do not contain gluten. Gluten-containing ingredients such as wheat, barley and rye will be highlighted in bold on the product's label. Manufacturers may also indicate whether there is a chance that their product may have been accidentally contaminated with gluten during the manufacturing process.

SmartPoints® have been calculated using the values for generic foods, not brands (except where stated). Tracking using branded items may affect the recorded SmartPoints.

WHEN YOU SEE THESE SYMBOLS:

 Tells you how many SmartPoints are in the recipe.

 Indicates a recipe is suitable for freezing.

 Indicates a No Count recipe.

GF Indicates a recipe is gluten free or can be made gluten free with a few simple swaps, for example by using gluten free soy sauce.

V Indicates a recipe is vegetarian.

Seven ᶜᵌ

Produced by Seven Publishing on behalf of Weight Watchers International, Inc. Published January 2018. All rights reserved. No part of this publication may be reproduced, stored in a retrieval system or transmitted in any form by any means, electronic, mechanical photocopying, recording or otherwise, without the prior written permission of Seven Publishing. First published in Great Britain by Seven Publishing Ltd.

Seven Publishing Ltd, 3-7 Herbal Hill, London EC1R 5EJ
www.seven.co.uk

This book is copyright under the Berne Convention. No reproduction without permission. All rights reserved.

10 9 8 7 6 5 4 3 2 1

© 2018 Weight Watchers International, Inc. All rights reserved. The SmartPoints Weight-Loss System and these materials are proprietary to Weight Watchers International, Inc. and are licensed to Weight Watchers members solely for their personal use in losing and controlling their weight. Any other use, including but not limited to reproduction or distribution in any form or medium, is strictly prohibited. NOT FOR RESALE. WEIGHT WATCHERS, POINTS and SmartPoints are the registered trademarks of Weight Watchers International, Inc.

A CIP catalogue record for this book is available from the British Library. ISBN: 978-0-9935835-8-2

WEIGHT WATCHERS PUBLICATIONS TEAM
Samantha Rees, Stephanie Williams, Ruby Bamford, Nicola Kirk, Nicola Hill

FOR SEVEN PUBLISHING LTD
FOOD
Food editor Sarah Akhurst
Food assistants Linzi Brechin, Nadine Brown, Gabriella English
Nutritionist Alexandra Harris

EDITORIAL
Editor-in-Chief Helen Renshaw
Editor Ward Hellewell **Sub-editors** Christine Faughlin, Chloe Hay

DESIGN & PHOTOGRAPHY
Art director Liz Baird
Photography Dan Jones
Food stylist Sarah Cook
Prop stylist Tonia Shuttleworth
Hair and make-up Jo Clayton

ACCOUNT MANAGEMENT
Account manager Gina Cavaciuti
Group publishing director Kirsten Price

PRODUCTION
Production director Sophie Dillon
Colour reproduction by F1 Colour
Printed in Italy by Rotolito Lombarda

Contents

Welcome to the Weight Watchers Flex Cookbook. In this book, you'll find a collection of delicious, simple recipes created by the Weight Watchers *kitchen team* – Sarah, Nadine and Linzi. Many of the recipes have have been specifically designed around *zero Points foods*, so that you can use them as the foundation to build your *everyday meals*, adding extras, side dishes and even snacks and desserts when you fancy. Weight Watchers Flex is all about choice – no food is off limits – and this book will *inspire you* with ideas of how to be *creative* with your SmartPoints budget. Plus, we've included some *meal plans* to show how easy it is to plan ahead, enjoy the foods you love and still lose weight.

Shopping, cooking & eating

ALL ABOUT SMARTPOINTS

With SmartPoints, all foods are on the menu, helping you to have a balanced diet and still enjoy the foods you love.

All of the recipes in this book have been specially designed for Weight Watchers Flex, making it easy for you to enjoy fabulous food while on your weight-loss journey.

If you're new to SmartPoints, don't worry – it's easy. When you join Weight Watchers, you're given a SmartPoints budget and it's completely up to you what you do with it. Each day you can rollover up to 4 unused

SmartPoints from your daily allowance and add them into your weeklies – perfect if you have a night out at a restaurant, a special celebration meal or a weekend takeaway planned – and you reset each weigh-in day.

ZERO POINTS FOODS

All foods have a SmartPoints value – but lots of foods are zero SmartPoints and you can use these without weighing, measuring

*Available to meetings and online subscribers.

or tracking them. Use them to get the most out of your SmartPoints budget.

You don't need to keep track of zero Points foods – you can just enjoy them until you are comfortably full. The zero Points food list includes most fruits and vegetables, many plant-based proteins, skinless chicken and turkey breast, hen eggs, unsmoked fish and seafood, pulses and fat-free yogurt, so there are plenty of versatile ingredients you can use as a starting point for delicious meals (for the full list, see page 14).

FOOD WITH FREEDOM

It's up to you how you use your SmartPoints budget – that's what makes Weight Watchers so flexible. You can choose to base your meals around zero Points foods, and then spend your allowance on side dishes, desserts, or snacks throughout the day. Or you can use your budget on more indulgent meals that are a bit higher in SmartPoints. If you want to sprinkle Parmesan cheese on your pasta, or have a crusty roll with your soup, no problem. Or if you fancy a glass of wine with your meal, that's okay too – as long as you stick to your

SmartPoints budget, you're free to spend it on whatever you like.

Keeping track of your SmartPoints is important, and it's easy to do. All the recipes in this book have their SmartPoints values included, and wherever we've suggested added extras, ingredient swaps or side dishes, we've shown whether these have SmartPoints too.

You can also find out the SmartPoints values of most foods, including supermarket products and restaurant meals, by going online to weightwatchers.co.uk, or using the Weight Watchers app*.

ZERO POINTS FOODS

All these foods are zero SmartPoints, so you can enjoy them without tracking and use them as a base of lots of tasty meals.

DAIRY & EGGS
Hen eggs
Yogurt, fat-free, plain
(including Greek & Skyr)
Yogurt, soya, plain

FISH & SHELLFISH
All unsmoked fish & shellfish –
fresh, frozen or tinned in water,
including, but not limited to:
Fresh & prepared:
Bream, red or black
Cockles
Cod
Cod roe
Coley
Crab
Crayfish
Dover sole
Eel
Eels, jellied
Grouper
Haddock
Hake
Halibut
Herring
Hoki
John Dory
King prawns
Lemon sole
Lobster
Mackerel
Monkfish
Mullet, grey
Mullet, red
Mussels
Octopus
Orange roughy
Oysters
Pike
Plaice
Pollock
Prawns
Rainbow trout

Red snapper (Red sea bream)
Rock salmon (Dog fish)
Roll mop herring
Salmon
Sardines
Scallops
Sea bass
Sea bream
Seafood selection
Shark
Shrimps
Skate
Soft herring roe
Sprats
Squid
Swordfish
Tiger prawns
Tilapia
Trout
Tuna
Turbot
Whelks
Whiting
Winkles
Tinned:
Caviar in brine, drained
Clams in brine, drained
Cockles in vinegar
Crab in brine
Mackerel in brine
Pilchards in brine, drained
Pink salmon
Red salmon
Sardines in brine, drained
Tuna in brine, drained
Tuna in springwater, drained

POULTRY
Cooked deli:
Chicken breast, wafer- thin
Turkey breast, wafer-thin
Fresh & Prepared:
Chicken breast mince
Chicken breast, skinless
Turkey breast mince
Turkey breast, skinless

FRUIT & VEGETABLES
All fruit – fresh, frozen or tinned
in natural juice or water, drained
Most vegetables fresh, frozen or
tinned without oil or sugar – see
page 16 for exceptions.

ALL LEGUMES
Fresh, frozen or tinned without
oil or sugar, including, but not
limited to:
Aduki beans
Beansprouts
Black eyed beans
Borlotti beans
Broad beans
Butter beans
Cannellini beans
Chickpeas
Flageolet beans
French-style
Fresh beans
Green
Haricot beans
Kidney beans
Lentils, brown
Lentils, green
Lentils, split red
Mung beans
Pinto beans
Runner
Soya beans
Tinned beans
Yellow split peas

MEAT-FREE PROTEIN SUBSTITUTE
Plain tofu
Quorn fillet
Quorn mince
Quorn pieces

'Using zero Points foods to *build meals* means you can enjoy lots of lovely added *extras* too.' NADINE

EVERYDAY FOODS & THEIR SMARTPOINTS

No food is off-limits when you join Weight Watchers – but not all foods are equal in SmartPoints. This at-a-glance guide shows some frequently eaten foods, with their SmartPoints values, to make it easier for you to track them.

BREAD & CEREALS

Bagel 80g	6
Bread roll, 60g	4
Calorie-controlled white bread, 1 slice	1
Cornflakes, 30g	3
Crumpet, 60g	4
English muffin, 70g	5
Muesli (no added sugar or salt), 50g	6
Oats, 30g	3
Pitta bread, 60g	4
Rice crispies, 30g	4
Scone, fruit or plain, 60g	8
Tortilla wrap, 42g	4

VEGETABLES

Avocado, ½ medium, 77.5g	5
Olives, in brine, 10 olives, 30g	1
Mushy peas, 100g	2
Parsnip, 90g	2
Plantain, 180g	7
Potato, 200g	5
Sweet potato, 150g	5
Yam, 150g	5

MEAT

Chorizo, 3 slices, 15g	2
Corned beef, 35g slice	2
Bacon, 2 medallions, 40g	1
Frankfurter, 47g	5
Ham, wafer thin, 2 slices	1
Salami, 11g slice	2
Sausage, pork, 20g	2

SIDES

Baked potato, 200g	8
Baked beans, 3 tablespoons	3
Chips (chip shop), 240g	18
Coleslaw (readymade), 1 tablespoon	3
Guacamole, 1 tablespoon	1
Houmous, 1 tablespoon	3
Pasta, fresh, uncooked, 80g	6
Potato salad (readymade), 125g	6
Rice, uncooked, 60g	6
Salsa, fresh, no oil, 1 tablespoon	0
Sweet potato, 150g	5

SPREADS & SAUCES

Brown sauce, 2 tablespoons	2
Butter, 1 teaspoon	2
Chilli sauce, 2 tablespoons	1
Chocolate nut spread, 1 heaped teaspoon	2
Honey, 1 heaped teaspoon, 8g	1
Jam, 1 heaped teaspoon, 18g	3
Ketchup, 2 tablespoons	2
Low-fat spread, 1 teaspoon	1
Mayonnaise, 1 teaspoon	1
Mustard, coarse grain, 1 heaped teaspoon	1
Peanut butter, 15g	3
Salad cream, 1 tablespoon, 15g	2

DRINKS

Beer, 1 pint	7
Cider, dry, 1 pint	9
Cola, 330ml	8
Coconut water, 330ml	3
Drinking chocolate, 1 tablespoon	4
Dry white wine, 175ml	5
Fruit juice squash, 30ml	1
G&T, 25ml gin, 150ml tonic	4
Milk, semi-skimmed, 142ml	3
Orange juice, unsweetened, 250ml	5
Red wine, 175ml	4
Soya milk, unsweetened, 142ml	1

SNACKS & DESSERTS

Almonds, 6, 13g	2
Cheese, Cheddar, 40g	6
Cheese, half-fat Cheddar, 40g	3
Chocolate, 4 squares, 28g	8
Custard, 150g pot	7
Custard Cream biscuit, 12g	3
Digestive biscuit, 13g	2
Ice cream, vanilla, 1 scoop	5
Peanuts, plain unsalted, 25g	4
Popcorn, plain, popped without oil, 25g	3
Potato crisps, salted, 32.5g bag	5
Meringue nest, 12g	3
Sultanas, 30g	5
Tortilla chips, 30g bag	5
Yogurt, fat-free fruit, 150g	4

'Use *zero* **Points** foods as fillings in your sandwiches and wraps, and all you have to **count** is the bread!' LINZI

MEAL PLANNING & SHOPPING

Planning meals in advance and shopping smarter make staying on track that much easier. Here's how to do it…

The way you shop and plan your meals can make all the difference when it comes to staying on track and eating a balanced diet. By planning ahead, you take the guesswork out of what you're eating and can feel confident that you'll stay on track all week long. Getting organised will not only help you to keep within your SmartPoints allowance, but it will help you to stay positive, focused and in control. Follow our easy tips to make meal planning and shopping work for you.

1 STOCK UP

Before you start your meal planning, make sure you have a well-stocked storecupboard and freezer. Decant dry ingredients such as oats, pasta and rice into clearly labelled airtight containers – they'll keep longer and you'll be able to see at a glance exactly what you've got. Next, stock up on staple ingredients that you'll use time and again – not just for making the recipes in this book, but for any meals you regularly make. Having things like frozen veg, dried herbs and spices, packs of pasta, grains and pulses, and cooking essentials such as oil, calorie controlled cooking spray and stock cubes, means you'll be able to create a tasty meal even when the fridge is bare.

2 MAKE A MEAL PLAN

It may seem like a bit of work up front, but creating a meal plan will save you time and money further down the line. First, brainstorm ideas, look up recipes, check what you have in your storecupboard and freezer and think about how you want to use your SmartPoints that week. Save more complicated meals for the days when you have more time and less pressure. For busier evenings, plan to make recipes that won't require lots of ingredients or lengthy prep time in the kitchen. See page 206 for some ideas.

3 CHECK YOUR CUPBOARDS

Once you've figured out what you're going to cook for the week, write a list based on what you need and what you already have. Our Shop guide (available in meetings and at the Weight Watchers online shop) can help you with this. It will stop you from doubling up on items you already have and encourage you to use fresh ingredients nearing their use by date.

4 STICK TO YOUR SHOPPING LIST

A grocery list will certainly help you to buy only what you need for the week, but even when you have one, it can be hard to resist the temptation to add extra items to your trolley as your browse the aisles. One trick to avoid making impulse purchases is to write your list in aisle order – that way you'll only visit the sections of the supermarket you need, rather than going back and forth and passing all those items you're hoping to steer clear of. Alternatively, try online grocery shopping – you'll not only avoid common supermarket pitfalls, but most sites will remember your regular shops or commonly bought items, so you can simply repeat your core shop with small tweaks and additions, week after week.

5 KEEP THINGS INTERESTING

At first, you might think that meal planning is the opposite of cooking creatively, but keeping things interesting doesn't have to mean being spontaneous in the kitchen. Avoid mealtime monotony by repurposing leftovers into quick new meals or lunches, rather than just simply reheating a portion at a later date. For example, if you make a Bolognese sauce on a Monday, plan to use it in another simple meal, like a stuffed jacket potato, later in the week. And, if you make a roast chicken on a Sunday, turn the leftovers into a tasty chicken salad for Monday's lunch.

6 DON'T COOK SEPARATE MEALS

Whether you're the one who's following the plan, or someone in your family is, cooking separate meals for everyone might seem like the only option. But instead of cooking multiple dishes, save time by planning meals that everyone can eat, and then adapt them as necessary. For example, you can make a pasta sauce that everyone will enjoy but serve some with pasta and some with courgetti. Similarly, a pot of soup can be served with a sandwich made with regular bread for some and Weight Watchers bread for others. Involve the rest of the family in meal planning too – it can alleviate some of the pressure of coming up with new ideas, and it will get everyone excited about mealtimes. Consider introducing a theme night – such as pizza Friday or taco Tuesday. This will help to keep meal planning simple, while still offering plenty of variety at the same time.

7 KEEP COSTS LOW

Make your budget stretch further by buying staples, such as pasta and rice, in bulk and storing them in airtight containers to keep them fresh. Similarly, keep a supply of frozen fruit, veg and herbs on hand so you can use exactly the amount you need, without any waste. Buying larger joints of meat and whole birds and fish is cheaper than getting pre-prepared cuts too, and you can portion them yourself.

8 BATCH COOKING AND FREEZING

Your freezer will soon become your new best friend when you're planning meals for the week ahead. First step is to fill your freezer with homemade ready meals for those nights you don't have time to cook. You can do this by making double or triple batches of soups, stews, casseroles, pasta sauces and curries and freezing in individual portions. Label each dish with its name and the date you froze it, and store newer dishes towards the back of the freezer so you eat the older ones first. Another time-saving trick is to chop and freeze veggies – such as onions, carrots, celery, peppers, broccoli and cauliflower – or buy pre-chopped to speed up weeknight meal-prep. It's a great way to stop fresh veg from being wasted too.

Tip

Assembly cooking is perfect for busy weekdays. Use leftovers or ready-to-eat ingredients, such as tuna, to put together super-quick, healthy meals.

COOKING & EATING

Cooking from scratch means you know exactly what you and your family are eating. Make it easy, enjoyable and rewarding with these simple tips…

Creating healthy, nutritious meals to help you on your get-healthy journey is as much about how you cook as what you cook. Whether it's finding the right ingredients, prepping efficiently or cooking cleverly, our tips for cooking and eating will help you deliver exciting meals you'll never tire of making.

1 TAKE A SEASONAL APPROACH

Eating foods when they're in season makes perfect sense. Not only are they at their very best, they're plentiful and cheaper to buy too. Supermarkets stock their shelves with most produce all year round, but you'll know when it's in season by keeping an eye on prices. Outside the supermarket, local farmers and food markets are a good place to discover more about what's in season – stroll around (think of the FitPoints!™) and chat to the growers and farmers directly. They'll be brimming with knowledge and passion about the seasonal items they're selling, and will likely give you lots of tips for how best to enjoy what they've got on offer.

2 BOOST FLAVOUR WITHOUT ADDING SMARTPOINTS

There was once a time where boosting the flavour of the food you were cooking and eating came down to adding lots of salt, butter or sugar. These days, getting your hands on healthy and interesting flavour boosters is easier than ever. Fresh and dried herbs are ideal for elevating a plain dish to something more interesting. Poaching and cooking foods in a little low-salt stock is another way to bring out the flavour. Spice rubs and marinades can jazz up fillets of meat, fish and poultry, while sauces and accompaniments, such as soy sauce, fish sauce, Worcestershire sauce, mustards and flavoured vinegars are all

easy ways to bring another flavour dimension to meals, without adding any SmartPoints. Don't be afraid of trying unfamiliar ingredients – mirin, miso and pomegranate molasses might sound exotic, but they're all readily available and will help you add interesting flavours and create lots of variety at mealtimes.

3 KEEP MEALS VARIED AND INTERESTING

Once you have a repertoire of recipes in place, it can be all too easy to fall into the habit of cooking the same things day in day out, which can get boring. There are lots of fun ways to keep meals interesting. For example, there's a wealth of zero-hero fresh fruit and vegetables to choose from, so try not to default to familiar ingredients you're in the habit of buying (and cooking). Challenge yourself in the supermarket to buy one new thing you've never tried before, and then research how to prepare and cook it. You could also involve the rest of your family in your cooking plans as they might just have an idea that you would never have thought of.

Or why not try to find some completely new recipes (either from this book or from any other source) and commit to cooking a different one every week. Make it even more fun by getting the family to give it a score out of 10 at the end of the meal. Finally, when it comes to cooking your favourite go-to recipes, see if you can swap out ingredients to make the dish a little more fresh and exciting. Some recipes lend themselves to easy adaptation, such as fish pie. You could swap potato mash for celeriac mash, experiment with different fish and shellfish, and boost the sauce with herbs, spices and mustards. These simple tweaks won't require any specialist cooking skills or knowledge, but will transform your weekly meals and may even reduce the SmartPoints values.

'*Cooking* from scratch gives you so much more *choice* and control over what you're *eating*.' SARAH

your breakfast for the following morning. Weigh out oats, cereals, and grains, measure out milk and juices, and for cooked breakfasts, prepare vegetables and other ingredients so that they're good to go. For breakfasts to eat on the go, prep bircher muesli or overnight oats before going to bed and grab them on your way out the door, or spend some time on a Sunday making cereal bars that will last the week (see page 182).

7 SAVE TIME IN THE KITCHEN

When you want a healthy meal on the table in next to no time, the equipment and techniques you use in the kitchen can all help. Nonstick pans not only reduce the amount of oil you need to cook with, but also heat up in seconds and are easy to wash. Use microwaves to steam-cook veg from scratch or partially cook veg for baking or roasting. Stick blenders allow you to blend soups and sauces in the same pan you cooked them in, while a pair of kitchen scissors can be used to quickly snip fresh herbs straight into the pan, trim fat from meat, and cut ham and bacon into strips. Even your electric kettle will help. Rather than waiting for water to boil on the hob, boil it in your kettle in a flash, then pour it into a pan, turn the heat to high and let it come back to a boil – it will take seconds.

4 HERO THE NEW ZERO POINTS INGREDIENTS

Our zero Points foods (see page 14) include most fruit and veg, lean proteins, pulses and dairy options. Aim to use at least one of these as the base of most of your meals, and then build a recipe around it using added extras.

5 CONTROL YOUR PORTIONS

Once you know what you're going to be cooking and eating, figuring out how much to eat is your next step. Many people find portion size hardest to calculate, so it can be a good idea to start weighing some food and measuring drinks. Once you become familiar with certain foods and recipes, you might find yourself able to 'guesstimate' portion sizes instead. Just take care to track the portion you are actually eating, rather than the default serving size suggestion.

6 WAKE UP TO EASY BREAKFASTS

It's easy enough to be creative when it comes to evening meals, but coming up with new breakfast ideas can be more of a challenge, especially when you have the pressures of time. Planning ahead for breakfasts is just as crucial as it is for evening meals. Before you go to bed each night, prepare

8 EAT OUT AND STAY ON TRACK

We all need a break from cooking every now and then. That weekend brunch with the family, café date with friends, or restaurant dining with your other half – you can do it all and stay on track with just a bit of forward thinking. If, for example, you know you're going out for dinner, keep your breakfast, lunch and snacks for that same day close to zero SmartPoints and use your daily allowance for the restaurant meal. And don't forget to use your weeklies – that's what they're there for. You can roll over up to 4 unused SmartPoints from each day's allowance into your weeklies. Look at the restaurant's menu ahead of time and work out what you're going to eat. Many have nutritional details of each dish available on their website so you can work out the SmartPoints in advance (or consult the *Eat Out* guide). If the occasion is impromptu, choose wisely from the menu (go for veg-based dishes and lean proteins). Don't be afraid to ask if you can customise dishes too – swapping chips for salad and asking for meat grilled rather than fried will help keep SmartPoints low.

'**No Count** is a great option if you're really *busy* and don't feel like tracking.' SARAH

NO COUNT

Don't think tracking SmartPoints every day is for you? Then give No Count a go.
There's no measuring or tracking involved and you don't have to worry about portion sizes either – so long as you stick to the foods on the No Count list, you can eat as much as you like, until you are comfortably full.

The No Count list is made up of lots of your favourite foods, including most fruits and vegetables, lean meats, fish and grains as well as several flavour boosters, so it's simple to create absolutely delicious meals that will fit into your healthy-eating plan. All of the No Count recipes in this book are marked with a green circle, and many more of the recipes can be easily adapted to make them No Count too. For example, if a recipe calls for white rice you can substitute brown rice, and if it calls for beef mince, just make sure you use extra lean. For those recipes that you simply can't adapt to make No Count, you have a weekly SmartPoints allowance that you can dip into.

Your weeklies are there so you never have to miss out on your favourite foods – even if they're not on the No Count foods list – so don't be afraid to use them! Even if you do normally track SmartPoints, you can still have the occasional No Count day. This is a great option for when you're really busy and don't feel like tracking, or if you're on holiday and are unable to work out the SmartPoints for certain foods. No Count is also brilliant for entertaining. Buffets and sharing platters can make over-indulging all too easy and SmartPoints hard to track, but if you cook up a No Count feast, you can dig in and enjoy yourself worry free. And if you're concerned your guests won't enjoy No Count foods, you'll be happy to know that homemade burgers, potato wedges and fat-free frozen yogurt all make the cut. Who wouldn't be happy with that?

Eggs & dairy

EGGS BENEDICT BRUNCH

Our version of the classic brunch dish features a short-cut, healthier hollandaise.

Serves 4

PREP TIME 5 minutes
COOK TIME 15 minutes

Ingredients

8 bacon medallions
6 plum tomatoes, halved
1 teaspoon dried parsley, plus
  an extra pinch, to serve
2 teaspoons white wine vinegar
3 tablespoons reduced-fat
  mayonnaise
1 tablespoon Dijon mustard
Juice of ½ lemon
4 large eggs
2 English muffins, halved
  and toasted
Pinch of paprika, to serve

 SmartPoints
4 per serving

Method

1 Preheat the oven to 200°C, fan 180°C, gas mark 6 and
  line a baking sheet with baking paper. Put the bacon
  and tomato halves on the prepared baking sheet, then
  season the tomatoes to taste and scatter over the dried
  parsley. Bake for 10 minutes, then turn the bacon
  medallions over and cook for another 2-3 minutes
  until they are golden and the tomatoes are tender.

2 Meanwhile, bring a large pan of water to a gentle simmer
  and add 1 teaspoon of the vinegar. In a small bowl, whisk
  the remaining vinegar into the mayonnaise with the
  mustard and lemon juice, then season to taste. If you
  need to, add a splash of water to make the hollandaise
  thin enough to drizzle.

3 Poach the eggs, one at a time, in the simmering water for
  3 minutes until set, then remove from the water with a
  slotted spoon and drain on kitchen paper. When all the
  eggs are cooked, remove the pan from the heat and return
  all 4 eggs to the water for 15 seconds to warm through.

4 Top each muffin half with 2 bacon medallions and a
  poached egg. Drizzle with the hollandaise, scatter over
  the extra parsley and the paprika, then serve with the
  roasted tomatoes.

 ## HARISSA
Fancy a spicier sauce? Stir 2 teaspoons of
harissa into the hollandaise instead of the
Dijon mustard for no additional **SmartPoints**.

 ## ROASTED BROCCOLI
Add some super greens to your brunch by
serving this with roasted broccoli (p51), for
an extra **2 SmartPoints** per serving.

Eggs & Dairy

MEXICAN-STYLE SCRAMBLED EGGS

This recipe turns ordinary scrambled eggs into something much more special.

Serves 4
PREP TIME 15 minutes
COOK TIME 5 minutes

Ingredients
6 large eggs
100ml skimmed milk
1 teaspoon mild chilli powder
2 teaspoons sunflower oil
Handful fresh coriander,
  roughly chopped
4 taco shells, warmed to
  pack instructions

For the salsa
4 spring onions, white and
  green parts separated, then
  both thinly sliced
4 tomatoes, finely diced
1 tablespoon jalapeno slices,
  drained and finely chopped
Juice of 1 lime, plus lime wedges,
  to serve

 SmartPoints
3 per serving

 See page 6

Method

1 To make the salsa, combine the white parts of the spring onions, the tomatoes, jalapenos and lime juice in bowl. Season to taste and set aside.

2 Put the eggs in a jug with the milk and chilli powder and beat together with a fork. Season to taste.

3 Brush a large non-stick pan with the oil and put over a low heat. Pour in the egg mixture and leave for 30 seconds, then fold in from the edges as it starts to set. Stir with a wooden spoon every now and then, letting more of the egg set between stirring. Continue until the eggs are softly set, then remove from the heat. Stir in the green parts of the spring onions and the coriander.

4 Spoon the scrambled eggs into the warm taco shells and top with the salsa, then serve with the lime wedges.

 ### AVOCADO SALSA
Instead of the basic salsa, try serving this with avocado salsa (p52) for a total of **8 SmartPoints** per serving.

 ### FETA
Stir 100g crumbled light feta into the eggs with the coriander and green spring onion parts, for an extra **2 SmartPoints** per serving.

 ### BLACK BEANS
Drain and rinse a 400g tin of black beans then spoon on top of the eggs along with the salsa, for no additional **SmartPoints**.

Eggs & Dairy

ROASTED TOMATO CRUSTLESS QUICHE

Full of flavour and sweetness, roasted tomatoes top this easy egg dish.

Serves 4
PREP TIME 10 minutes
COOK TIME 40 minutes

Ingredients
250g cherry tomatoes on the vine
2 teaspoons olive oil
1 onion, diced
2 mixed peppers, deseeded
  and diced
10 fresh basil leaves, torn
25g vegetarian Italian hard cheese,
  finely grated
6 large eggs
150ml skimmed milk
1 tablespoon tomato purée

SmartPoints
2 per serving

V **GF** See page 6

Method

1 Preheat the oven to 180°C, fan 160°C, gas mark 4, and line a 20-22cm round pie dish or cake tin with a sheet of baking paper. Chop 50g of the tomatoes and set aside the remaining tomatoes (leave them on their stems).

2 Heat the oil in a medium pan over a low heat and cook the onion for 6-8 minutes until soft.

3 Add the peppers and cook for 1 minute, then add the chopped cherry tomatoes and cook for 1 minute. Remove from the heat and stir in the basil.

4 In a medium bowl, whisk together the grated cheese, eggs, milk and tomato purée, then season to taste. Stir in the onion and pepper mixture, then pour everything into the prepared pie dish. Bake for 25 minutes, then top with the remaining cherry tomatoes and bake for 5 minutes, or until the quiche is set and the tomatoes are tender. Serve hot, warm or cold, cut into wedges.

Add ### GOAT'S CHEESE
5 minutes before you add the vine tomatoes to the top of the quiche, crumble over 50g soft goat's cheese. This will add **2 SmartPoints** per serving.

Side ### SKINNY COLESLAW
Try serving this with skinny coleslaw (p52) for no additional **SmartPoints** per serving.

4 QUICK YOGURT IDEAS

Perfect for sweet and savoury dishes, 0% fat natural Greek yogurt is one of those ingredients to always keep in your fridge on stand-by. Great for instant puds and breakfasts, cooling down curries, livening up salads, or simply dunking veggies into – here are some of our favourite ideas.

MANGO LASSI
Makes 1
PREP TIME 5 minutes

Put 150g **0% fat natural Greek yogurt**, 75g ripe **mango** flesh, 1 teaspoon clear **honey** and a pinch of **ground cardamom** in a blender, along with 5 ice cubes. Whizz until smooth, then add a squeeze of **lime juice** and serve. This cooling, refreshing drink goes well with spicy dishes, such as curries.

 **SmartPoints**
6 per lassi   See page 6

TZATZIKI
Serves 4
PREP TIME 10 minutes

Deseed and coarsely grate ½ **cucumber**, then mix with 200g **0% fat natural Greek yogurt**, 2 teaspoons **dried mint**, 1 teaspoon **dried dill**, 2 crushed **garlic cloves** and 2 teaspoons **white wine vinegar**, and season to taste. Use as a dip, or serve with spicy meats such as jerk chicken or kebabs.

 SmartPoints
0 per serving    See page 6

BEETROOT DIP
Serves 4
PREP TIME 10 minutes

Coarsely grate 125g cooked **beetroot** and set aside. Put another 125g cooked beetroot into a food processor with 100g **0% natural Greek yogurt**, 2 teaspoons **pomegranate molasses**, 1 tablespoon **lemon juice**, 1 crushed **garlic clove** and 1½ teaspoons **cumin seeds**. Season to taste, then whizz until smooth. Pulse in a small handful of roughly chopped **fresh mint** leaves. Put the dip in a serving bowl and stir through the grated beetroot. Serve topped with ½ teaspoon **cumin seeds** and more fresh mint leaves. This is great with crudités or toasted wholemeal pitta bread.

 SmartPoints
0 per serving   See page 6

RANCH-STYLE DRESSING
Serves 8
PREP TIME 5 minutes

Put 100g **0% fat natural Greek yogurt**, 2 tablespoons **reduced-fat mayonnaise**, 1 crushed **garlic clove**, ½ teaspoon English **mustard powder**, 1 teaspoon **dried onion granules** and 1 teaspoon **dried dill** in a food processor with 3 tablespoons water. Whizz to a smooth dressing, then stir in 1 tablespoon snipped fresh **chives** and 1 tablespoon chopped **fresh flat-leaf parsley**. This is enough to dress a salad to serve 8 people and will keep in the fridge in a sealed jar for up to 3 days.

 SmartPoints
0 per serving    See page 6

BLUE CHEESE & PEAR TOAST

Sharp blue cheese and sweet pears combine perfectly in this simple dish.

Serves 4
PREP TIME 5 minutes
COOK TIME 3 minutes

Ingredients
3 ripe pears
Juice of ½ lemon
25g low-fat soft cheese
75g Stilton, crumbled
4 slices Weight Watchers
  Thick Sliced Wholemeal Bread
25g rocket

 SmartPoints
6 per serving

Method

1 Halve, core and slice the pears into thin wedges, then put in a small bowl and toss with half the lemon juice to stop them from turning brown. Set aside.

2 In a small bowl, mix the soft cheese with 15g of the Stilton and the remaining lemon juice, then season to taste.

3 Toast the bread in a toaster or under the grill. Spread with the soft cheese mixture, then top with the rocket and pear. Crumble over the remaining Stilton, then serve.

 PARMA HAM
Lay 1 slice of lean Parma ham per person over the soft cheese spread before topping with the pears and rocket leaves for an extra **1 SmartPoint** per serving.

 SPINACH & PINE NUT SALAD
Make this more substantial by serving it with spinach & pine nut salad (p52), for an extra **3 SmartPoints** per serving.

ROASTED VEG IN YOGURT SAUCE

This Turkish-inspired recipe is a different way to serve roasted vegetables.

Serves 4
PREP TIME 15 minutes
COOK TIME 35 minutes

Ingredients
250g baby parsnips, peeled
  and larger ones halved lengthways
250g Chantenay carrots, trimmed,
  larger ones halved lengthways
300g cauliflower florets
2 small red onions, cut into wedges
1 tablespoon olive oil
1 teaspoon ground coriander
1 teaspoon coriander seeds
Juice of ½ lemon
Small handful fresh mint leaves
75g pomegranate seeds

For the sauce
150g 0% fat natural Greek yogurt
Juice of ½ lemon
2 garlic cloves, crushed
¼ teaspoon ground turmeric
2 teaspoons dried mint
1 teaspoon clear honey
Small handful fresh mint leaves

 SmartPoints
3 per serving

 See page 6

Method

1 Preheat the oven to 200°C, fan 180°C, gas mark 6. Bring a large pan of water to the boil, add the parsnips and cook for 1 minute, then add the carrots and cook for a further 1 minute. Finally, add the cauliflower and cook for 1 minute. Drain the vegetables, reserving a cup of the cooking water.

2 Put the parsnips, carrots and red onion in a large roasting tin and drizzle over the olive oil. Roast for 15 minutes, then add the cauliflower, ground coriander, coriander seeds and lemon juice to the tin. Toss everything together and roast for another 10 minutes.

3 Meanwhile, put all the sauce ingredients in a blender or food processor and whizz to a smooth sauce. Gradually blend in some of the reserved cooking water until the sauce reaches a drizzling consistency. Season to taste.

4 Put the roasted vegetables onto a platter. Drizzle over a little of the sauce and toss together to coat, then drizzle with the rest of the sauce and scatter over the mint leaves and the pomegranate seeds. This can be served hot or cold, but if you're serving it cold, allow the veg to cool before you add the sauce.

 ## PITTA BREAD
Serve with a toasted Weight Watchers pitta bread per person, for an extra **4 SmartPoints** per serving.

 ## HERBY BROWN RICE
You could also serve this with herby brown rice (p51) for an extra **5 SmartPoints** per serving.

5 FABULOUS FRITTATAS

If you've got eggs in the fridge, you've got a meal! Try these tasty ideas.

HERB & ONION
Serves 4

PREP TIME 5 minutes   **COOK TIME** 25 minutes

Heat 1 tablespoon **olive oil** in a non-stick ovenproof frying pan. Cook 1 large sliced **onion** over a medium heat for 6-8 minutes until soft. Beat 8 large **eggs**, season to taste and stir in 2 tablespoons chopped **fresh herbs** – parsley, dill, tarragon, chives and coriander all work well. Preheat the grill to high. Pour the egg mixture over the onions, stir gently to mix, then cook over a low heat for 8-10 minutes until almost set. Transfer to the grill for 3-5 minutes until set, then serve.

 SmartPoints
1 per serving   See page 6

SQUASH & SPINACH

Serves 4

PREP TIME 10 minutes **COOK TIME** 30 minutes

Cook 300g diced **butternut squash** in a pan of boiling water for 3-5 minutes until tender, then drain. Put 100g **spinach** into a microwave-safe bowl, cover and cook for 1 minute on high. Heat 1 tablespoon **olive oil** in a non-stick ovenproof frying pan over a medium heat. Add 1 diced **onion** and cook for 6-8 minutes until soft. Stir in 2 teaspoons **curry powder**, 1 teaspoon **cumin seeds** and 1 teaspoon ground **turmeric**, and cook for another 1 minute. Beat 8 large **eggs** and season to taste. Stir the spinach and squash into the onion, pour over the egg mixture, stir gently and cook over a low heat for 8-10 minutes until almost set. Preheat the grill to high. Transfer to the grill for 3-5 minutes until set, then serve.

2 SmartPoints value

SmartPoints
2 per serving Ⓞ Ⓥ ⒼⒻ See page 6

41

GOAT'S CHEESE & ASPARAGUS
Serves 4
PREP TIME 5 minutes **COOK TIME** 25 minutes

Blanch 200g **asparagus tips** for 1 minute in a pan of boiling water, then drain and set aside. Heat 1 tablespoon **olive oil** in a non-stick ovenproof frying pan. Cook 2 diced **onions** over a medium heat for 6-8 minutes until soft. Beat 8 large **eggs**, season to taste and stir in the grated zest of 1 **lemon**, 1 tablespoon chopped **fresh dill** and 50g crumbled rindless **goat's cheese**. Cut half the asparagus into small pieces and stir into the onions. Pour the egg mixture over the onion and asparagus, stir gently, then top with the whole asparagus spears. Cook over a low heat for 8-10 minutes until almost set. Preheat the grill to high. Scatter over another 50g goat's cheese and 2 teaspoons **pumpkin seeds**. Transfer to the grill for 3-5 minutes until the top is set, then serve.

 SmartPoints
4 per serving See page 6

CHORIZO & FETA
Serves 4
PREP TIME 5 minutes **COOK TIME** 25 minutes

Heat 1 tablespoon **olive oil** in a non-stick ovenproof frying pan over a medium heat. Cook 1 sliced **red onion** for 6-8 minutes until soft, then add 2 crushed **garlic cloves** and cook for 1 minute. Stir in 2 teaspoons **smoked paprika** and 2 teaspoons **dried parsley**. Beat 8 large **eggs**, season to taste, then stir in 2 diced slices of **chorizo**. Deseed and chop 1 **red chilli**, then stir half into the egg mixture. Pour the egg mixture over the onion mixture, stir gently, then cook over a low heat for 8-10 minutes until almost set. Preheat the grill to high. Top the frittata with 4 more chorizo slices, then scatter over 50g crumbled **light feta** and the remaining chilli. Transfer to the grill for 3-5 minutes until the top is set and the chorizo slices are crisp, then serve.

 SmartPoints
3 per serving See page 6

SALMON, PEA & LEMON

Serves 4

PREP TIME 5 minutes **COOK TIME** 25 minutes

Put 2 skinless **salmon fillets** in a microwave-safe dish, splash with a little water and cover. Microwave on high for 2½ minutes. Mist a non-stick ovenproof frying pan with calorie controlled cooking spray and put over a medium heat. Cook 1 diced **onion** for 6-8 minutes until soft. In a bowl, beat 8 large **eggs**, season and stir in the zest of 1 **lemon**, 2 teaspoons **Dijon mustard** and 2 tablespoons chopped **fresh flat-leaf parsley**. Stir 200g frozen **peas** into the onions; flake the salmon into chunks and add to the pan. Pour over the eggs, stir gently, then cook over a low heat for 8-10 minutes until almost set. Preheat the grill to high. Transfer the frittata to the grill for 3-5 minutes until the top is set. Mix another 1 tablespoon chopped parsley with 4 teaspoons **capers**, scatter over the frittata, then serve with lemon wedges.

 SmartPoints
0 per serving **GF** See page 6

KALE, PANCETTA & POACHED EGGS

A delicious twist on bacon and eggs! This warm salad couldn't be simpler.

Serves 4

PREP TIME 15 minutes
COOK TIME 20 minutes

Ingredients

8 slices pancetta
125g shredded kale
3 shallots, finely chopped
½ cucumber, diced
½ teaspoon English mustard powder
1 tablespoon extra virgin olive oil
2 tablespoons cider vinegar
1½ teaspoons yellow mustard seeds
1 teaspoon white wine vinegar
4 large eggs

 SmartPoints
3 per serving

 See page 6

Method

1 Preheat the oven to 180°C, fan 160°C, gas mark 4 and line a baking sheet with baking paper. Put the pancetta on the prepared baking sheet, then cook for 8-12 minutes until golden. Transfer to a plate to cool and crisp up, then break it into pieces.

2 Blanch the kale in boiling water for 1 minute, then drain and refresh under cold water. Combine the kale, shallots and cucumber in a large bowl and set aside. Put the mustard powder in a small bowl and stir in the oil to make a smooth paste. Whisk in the cider vinegar and 1 tablespoon water, then stir in the mustard seeds and set aside.

3 Bring a large pan of water to a gentle simmer and add the white wine vinegar. Poach the eggs, one at a time, in the simmering water for 3 minutes until set, then remove from the water with a slotted spoon and drain on kitchen paper. When all the eggs are cooked, remove the pan from the heat and return all 4 eggs to the water for 15 seconds to warm through.

4 Dress the kale salad with the mustard dressing, then divide it between 4 plates. Top with a poached egg and serve topped with the pancetta pieces.

 GARLIC & HERB BREADCRUMBS

For extra crunch, sprinkle garlic & herb breadcrumbs (p166) over the salad and poached eggs just before serving for an extra **2 SmartPoints** per serving.

 ROAST POTATOES

Try serving this with roast potatoes (p52) for an extra **5 SmartPoints** per serving.

CHEESE FONDUE WITH VEGGIE DIPPERS

For an easy, cheesy dinner that's made for sharing, try this fun fondue.

Serves 4
PREP TIME 10 minutes
COOK TIME 12 minutes

Ingredients
275ml skimmed milk
25g plain flour
1 teaspoon English
  mustard powder
100g half-fat extra mature
  Cheddar, grated
Vegetable crudités, to serve
  (try celery, carrots, radishes and
  blanched Tenderstem broccoli)

 **SmartPoints**
3 per serving

Method

1 Put the milk in a medium pan and whisk in the flour and mustard. Put over a medium heat and whisk continually while the milk comes to a gentle simmer. Reduce the heat to low and cook for 2-3 minutes, stirring constantly, until thickened.

2 Take the sauce off the heat and stir in the grated cheese, a handful at a time until it has melted. Season to taste and transfer the sauce to a fondue set if you have one, or an earthenware bowl, then serve immediately with the vegetable crudités for dipping.

 BOILED POTATOES
As well as the crudités, serve 50g boiled new potatoes per person, for an extra **1 SmartPoint** per serving.

GHERKINS
For a Scandinavian twist, serve 100g small gherkins along with the crudités for dipping, for no additional **SmartPoints**.

MEDITERRANEAN OMELETTE

An easy brunch dish filled with fresh tomatoes and courgettes.

Makes 1
PREP TIME 10 minutes
COOK TIME 10 minutes

Ingredients
3 eggs
100g courgette, grated
1 garlic clove, crushed
½ teaspoon smoked paprika
1 teaspoon dried oregano
2 teaspoons olive oil
1 large tomato, thickly sliced
4 pitted black olives, thinly sliced

 SmartPoints
3 per olmelette

  See page 6

Method

1 Lightly whisk the eggs in a mixing bowl. Stir in the courgette, garlic, paprika and oregano, then season to taste.

2 Heat the oil in a medium non-stick frying pan over a medium heat, then pour in the egg mixture. As the omelette cooks at the edges of pan, use a spatula to gently pull it towards the centre, tipping the pan slightly to allow more of the raw mixture to run to the edge. When the omelette has almost set, stop stirring and leave it on the heat for 2-3 minutes to finish cooking.

3 If you like the centre of your omelette a little soft, serve it immediately. If you prefer a firmer omelette, put it under a medium grill for 1 minute.

4 To serve, arrange the tomato slices over one half of the omelette and flip over the other half like a sandwich. Scatter with the sliced olives and serve in the pan, or transfer to a plate.

 ## BACON
Snip two bacon medallions into small pieces and fry in the oil in the frying pan before you add the egg mixture. When you tip in the egg mixture, stir straight away to mix the bacon through, then cook as above. This will add an extra **1 SmartPoint** per serving.

 ## SMOKED SALMON
Instead of bacon, try adding a slice of smoked salmon with the sliced tomatoes for an extra **2 SmartPoints** per serving.

Eggs & Dairy
SIDES

Healthy, easy side dishes that go perfectly
with our egg and dairy recipes.

Herby brown rice
+ 5 SmartPoints
per serving

Roasted broccoli
+ 2 SmartPoints
per serving

Spinach & pine nut salad
+ 3 SmartPoints
per serving

Skinny coleslaw
+ 0 SmartPoints
per serving

ROASTED BROCCOLI
Serves 4
PREP TIME 5 minutes
COOK TIME 20 minutes

Preheat the oven to 220°C, fan 200°C fan, gas mark 7, and line a baking sheet with baking paper. Toss 600g **broccoli** florets with 1 tablespoon **olive oil** and the juice of ½ **lemon**, then spread out on the prepared baking sheet and roast for 15 minutes. Scatter over 25g grated **vegetarian Italian hard cheese**, season to taste, then roast for another 3 minutes until the cheese is melted. Scatter over the grated zest of 1 **lemon** and serve immediately.

2 **SmartPoints**
SmartPoints value
2 per serving

V **GF** See page 6

HERBY BROWN RICE
Serves 4
PREP TIME 5 minutes
COOK TIME 20 minutes

Put 200g **brown rice** in a large pan of water. Sprinkle in 1 crumbled **vegetable stock cube**, bring to the boil and cook to pack instructions until the rice is tender. Drain well and stir through the grated zest and juice of 1 **lemon** and 4 tablespoons chopped **fresh herbs**, such as basil, coriander, flat-leaf parsley, dill and chives. Serve hot or cold.

5 **SmartPoints**
SmartPoints value
5 per serving

O **V** **GF** See page 6

SKINNY COLESLAW
Serves 4

PREP TIME 15 minutes

Whisk together 125g **0% fat natural yogurt**, the grated zest and juice of 1 **lemon**, 2 tablespoons **cider vinegar** and 2 tablespoons chopped **fresh coriander**. Season to taste. Shred half a **white cabbage** and put it into a serving bowl, along with 2 large grated **carrots** and 6 shredded **spring onions**. Drizzle over the dressing and mix well. Core 1 green eating **apple**, then cut into matchsticks. Stir through the salad just before serving.

 SmartPoints
0 per serving

  See page 6

SPINACH & PINE NUT SALAD
Serves 4

PREP TIME 5 minutes
COOK TIME 5 minutes

Toast 25g **pine nuts** in a dry frying pan over a low-medium heat until golden. Transfer to a bowl to cool. Put 3 small thinly sliced **shallots** in a small bowl, add 2 tablespoons **red wine vinegar**, 2 tablespoons **olive oil**, 2 teaspoons **wholegrain mustard** and 1 tablespoon **orange juice**. Whisk together to make a dressing. Put 80g young leaf **spinach** in a serving bowl, spoon over the dressing and toss to combine. Scatter over the toasted pine nuts to serve.

 SmartPoints
3 per serving

  See page 6

ROAST POTATOES
Serves 4

PREP TIME 5 minutes
COOK TIME 35 minutes

Preheat the oven to 200°C, fan 180°C fan, gas mark 6. Put 750g **new potatoes**, 4 teaspoons **sunflower oil** and the chopped leaves from 3 sprigs of **thyme** or **rosemary** (or a mixture) in a large roasting tin. Toss everything together, season to taste and roast for 20 minutes. Remove from the oven and add 6 unpeeled **garlic cloves** and 6 shredded **sage leaves** to the tin, then give everything a stir. Roast for 10-15 minutes until golden, then serve.

 SmartPoints
5 per serving

  See page 6

AVOCADO SALSA
Serves 4

PREP TIME 15 minutes

Halve, destone and peel 2 small **avocados**. Dice 3 of the halves and toss with 1 tablespoon **lime juice** in a bowl. Mash the remaining avocado with another 1 tablespoon of lime juice, then combine with the diced avocado, 2 tablespoons finely chopped **red onion**, 85g diced **tomatoes**, a handful of chopped **fresh coriander** leaves and enough **Tabasco** to suit your taste. Add 50g finely diced **watermelon**, then season to taste and serve with lime wedges to squeeze over.

 SmartPoints
5 per serving

  See page 6

Roast potatoes
+ 5 SmartPoints
per serving

Avocado salsa
+ 5 SmartPoints
per serving

Fish & Seafood

COCONUT-CRUSTED FISH FINGERS

Homemade fish fingers served with crushed peas and sweet potato chips.

Serves 4

PREP TIME 15 minutes
COOK TIME 40 minutes

Ingredients

75g white bread, torn into chunks
40g desiccated coconut
Calorie controlled cooking spray
600g sweet potatoes, peeled and
   cut into chips
1 tablespoon rapeseed oil
2 tablespoons plain flour, seasoned
1 egg, lightly beaten
500g skinless cod fillets, cut into
   thick fish fingers
300g peas
1 tablespoon reduced-fat
   mayonnaise
Handful fresh coriander,
   roughly chopped

 SmartPoints
12 per serving

Method

1 Preheat the oven to 200°C, fan 180°C, gas mark 6. Put the bread and coconut in a food processor and blitz until you have rough breadcrumbs. Spread them on a baking sheet and mist with cooking spray. Toast in the oven for around 10 minutes, or until lightly golden, then remove and set aside to cool.

2 Put the sweet potato chips in a roasting tin and drizzle over the oil. Toss to coat, then bake for 30 minutes, or until golden and cooked through.

3 Meanwhile, put the flour, egg and coconut breadcrumbs into three separate shallow bowls and mist a baking sheet with cooking spray. Dust each fish finger in the flour, then dip into the egg and roll in the crumbs to coat. Put the fish fingers on the prepared baking sheet and bake alongside the sweet potato chips for the final 15 minutes of cooking time.

4 While the fish and chips are cooking, boil the peas for 3-4 minutes. Drain and return to the pan. Add the mayonnaise and season to taste, then lightly crush with a potato masher. Stir through the coriander.

5 Serve the fish fingers with the sweet potato chips and peas on the side.

 BUTTERNUT SQUASH CHIPS
To lower the SmartPoints of this dish, use butternut squash to make the chips instead of sweet potato for a total of **7 SmartPoints** per serving.

 TARTARE SAUCE
Make this extra special by serving with tartare sauce (p80) for an extra **1 SmartPoint** per serving.

CELERIAC-TOPPED FISH PIE

A healthier version of the classic British dish that's bursting with flavour.

Serves 4

PREP TIME 20 minutes
COOK TIME 1 hour

Ingredients

1kg celeriac, peeled and cut
    into 2-3cm cubes
500ml semi-skimmed milk, plus
    an extra 2 tablespoons
400g smoked haddock fillets
400g unsmoked haddock fillets
1 small onion, halved
4 cloves
1 bay leaf
260g young leaf spinach
65g low-fat spread
50g plain flour
Small handful fresh dill,
    roughly chopped

 SmartPoints
7 per serving

Method

1 Preheat the oven to 200°C, fan 180°C, gas mark 6. Put the celeriac on a baking tray and roast for 35-40 minutes, until tender and golden.

2 Meanwhile, put 500ml milk in a large pan with the fish, onion, cloves and bay leaf. Bring to a simmer and poach for 4-5 minutes until the fish is just cooked. Use a slotted spoon to lift the fish from the milk and set aside. Remove the onion, cloves and bay leaf from the milk and discard, saving the poaching liquid.

3 Heat a splash of water in a wide pan, add the spinach and cook for 1-2 minutes until wilted. Remove from the pan, squeeze out any excess moisture and roughly chop.

4 Melt 50g of the low-fat spread in a large pan, then add the flour. Stir to make a paste, then cook for 2 minutes. Gradually add the poaching liquid, stirring to combine. Bring to a simmer and cook for 2 minutes, until the sauce thickens. Flake the cooked fish into large pieces and stir into the sauce, along with the cooked spinach and the dill. Season to taste.

5 Mash the roasted celeriac with the remaining low-fat spread and the 2 extra tablespoons milk, then season to taste.

6 Put the fish mixture into a baking dish and top with the mash. Bake for 20 minutes, until golden and bubbling.

 SQUASH & SWEET POTATO MASH
Instead of the celeriac mash, top this with squash & sweet potato mash (p80) for a total of **9 SmartPoints** per serving.

 PARMESAN CHEESE
Sprinkle 40g finely grated Parmesan over the top of the mash before baking for an extra **2 SmartPoints** per serving.

PRAWN KATSU BURGERS

These Japanese-style prawn burgers make a delicious change from meat.

Serves 2
PREP TIME 15 minutes, plus chilling
COOK TIME 8-10 minutes

For the burger
300g raw peeled king prawns
½ tablespoon cornflour
1 egg white
2 spring onions, trimmed and
    finely chopped
1 teaspoon fresh ginger, grated
50g panko breadcrumbs
2 teaspoons rapeseed oil
2 seeded burger buns
100g Savoy cabbage, finely
    shredded

For the katsu sauce
1½ tablespoons tomato ketchup
½ tablespoon Worcestershire sauce
1 teaspoon soy sauce
1 teaspoon mirin
½ teaspoon Dijon mustard
Pinch of garlic granules

 **SmartPoints**
10 per burger

Method

1 Put half the prawns in a food processor and blitz to a chunky paste. Roughly chop the remaining prawns and put in a bowl with the cornflour, egg white, spring onions, ginger and prawn paste. Mix well to combine, then shape into two burgers.

2 Put the panko breadcrumbs on a plate and press the burgers into the crumbs, until they are well coated. Chill for 30 minutes to firm up.

3 Heat the oil in a shallow non-stick frying pan and cook the burgers for 4-5 minutes on each side, until golden brown all over.

4 Meanwhile, whisk together all of the ingredients for the katsu sauce until smooth and combined.

5 Halve and toast the burger buns, and fill with the shredded cabbage, prawn patties and katsu sauce, then serve.

 ## WASABI MAYO
Like it spicy? Instead of the katsu sauce, mix ¼ teaspoon wasabi paste with 2 tablespoons reduced-fat mayonnaise. Spread over each side of the buns before adding the burgers, for a total of **11 SmartPoints** per serving.

 ## SPICY CHILLI CHIPS
For a side dish with a kick, try spicy chilli chips (p79). Add an extra **2 SmartPoints** per serving.

4 QUICK SALMON IDEAS

Steaming skinless salmon fillets is a quick and healthy way to cook them, and they can be used in lots of delicious ways…

SALMON & ASPARAGUS OMELETTE
Serves 1
PREP TIME 10 minutes **COOK TIME** 10 minutes

Blanch 70g **asparagus** for 2-3 minutes. Drain and chop. Mix with 1 steamed **salmon fillet**, flaked. In a jug, whisk 2 **eggs** with 1 tablespoon **semi-skimmed milk**. Add a handful of chopped fresh chives and season. Heat 1 teaspoon **vegetable oil** in a small frying pan. Pour in the eggs and cook for 3-4 minutes. Spoon the asparagus and salmon over one side, then fold. Cook for 1 minute to warm through, then serve.

 **SmartPoints**
2 per serving   See page 6

SALMON WITH SALSA VERDE
Serves 4
PREP TIME 10 minutes **COOK TIME** 15 minutes

For the salsa verde, blitz 1 **garlic clove**, 1 teaspoon **capers**, 4 small **gherkins**, a handful each of **fresh mint**, **parsley** and **basil**, 1 teaspoon Dijon mustard, 2 tablespoons **extra virgin olive oil**, 1 tablespoon **red wine vinegar** and the juice of ½ **lemon** in a food processor. Season to taste. Boil 600g **baby new potatoes** for 10 minutes and 300g **broccoli** for 5 minutes, then drain. Top 4 steamed **salmon fillets** with the salsa verde, and serve with the potatoes and broccoli.

 SmartPoints
5 per serving   See page 6

SALMON PITTAS
Serves 1
PREP TIME 5 minutes

Cut 1 wholemeal **pitta bread** in half and fill with **Little Gem lettuce** leaves and 1 steamed **salmon fillet**, flaked. Mix together 1 tablespoon **0% fat natural Greek yogurt**, 1 tablespoon reduced-fat **mayonnaise** and ½ teaspoon **harissa paste**. Spoon the harissa mayo into the pittas and serve.

 **SmartPoints**
5 per serving

SALMON CARBONARA
Serves 4
PREP TIME 15 minutes **COOK TIME** 15 minutes

Bring a pan of water to the boil and cook 300g **spaghetti** for 10-12 minutes. Mist a large frying pan with **calorie controlled cooking spray** and fry 2 trimmed, sliced **bacon medallions** for 4-5 minutes. Add 1 sliced **garlic clove** and cook for 1 minute. Meanwhile, in a small bowl, whisk together 2 **eggs** and 150g **0% fat natural Greek yogurt**. Drain the pasta, reserving the water. Put the spaghetti in the pan with the bacon and 100ml of the reserved pasta water. Stir, then add the egg mixture. Continue stirring off the heat until the pasta is coated in sauce. Flake through 2 steamed **salmon fillets**, a handful of chopped fresh **flat-leaf parsley** and 3 tablespoons grated **Parmesan**. Season to taste, then serve.

 **SmartPoints**
9 per serving

Fish & Seafood

SEA BASS FILLETS WITH CHORIZO CRUMB

A crispy, savoury breadcrumb mixture is the ideal topping for tender sea bass.

Serves 4
PREP TIME 10 minutes
COOK TIME 20 minutes

Ingredients
70g chorizo, diced
70g sourdough bread, torn into
   small pieces
Handful of fresh flat-leaf parsley,
   roughly chopped
Grated zest of 1 lemon
2 garlic cloves
4 x 90g sea bass fillets
500g fine green beans
Calorie controlled cooking spray
50g sun-dried tomatoes in oil,
   drained and chopped

5 SmartPoints
SmartPoints value 5 per serving

Method

1 Preheat the oven to 200°C, fan 180°C, gas mark 6 and line a baking sheet with baking paper. Fry the chorizo in a small frying pan over a medium heat for 3-4 minutes or until it starts to release oil. Transfer to a food processor with the bread, parsley, lemon zest and 1 of the garlic cloves. Blitz until you have a breadcrumb mixture.

2 Put the fish skin-side down on the prepared baking sheet and top with the chorizo crumb, pressing down so it sticks to the fish. Bake for 10-12 minutes.

3 Meanwhile, blanch the green beans in boiling water for 2-3 minutes until just tender, then drain and refresh under cold water. Mist a frying pan with cooking spray and put over a medium heat. Slice the remaining garlic clove and fry for 2 minutes. Add the beans and sun-dried tomatoes and cook for 3-4 minutes.

4 Serve the fish with the beans on the side.

CRISPY HERBED POTATO CUBES

In a roasting tin, toss 550g diced potatoes with 2 teaspoons rapeseed or olive oil and 1 teaspoon dried parsley. Season, then roast for 15-20 minutes at 200°C, fan 180°C, gas mark 6 until crispy and golden, for an extra **4 SmartPoints** per serving.

LEMON MAYO

This is great served with lemon mayo (p79), for an extra **2 SmartPoints** per serving.

COD & CHICKPEA CURRY

Spice up dinnertime with this fragrant fish curry, served with naan bread.

Serves 4
PREP TIME 10 minutes
COOK TIME 40 minutes

Ingredients
1 tablespoon rapeseed oil
2 red onions, finely sliced
2 garlic cloves, crushed
2cm-piece fresh ginger, grated
2 green chillies, deseeded
  and finely chopped
1 teaspoon mustard seeds
2 teaspoons ground turmeric
2 x 400g tins chopped tomatoes
400g tin chickpeas, drained
  and rinsed
500g cod loin, cut into large chunks
4 mini naan breads

SmartPoints
5 per serving

Method
1 Heat the oil in a large, deep frying pan over a medium heat and cook the onions for 6-8 minutes, or until soft. Add the garlic, ginger, chillies, mustard seeds and turmeric. Cook for 4-5 minutes, then add the tomatoes and chickpeas. Simmer for 15-20 minutes, until the tomatoes have reduced slightly.

2 Add the cod and cook for a further 5 minutes over a low heat until it is cooked through. Stir gently, taking care not to break up the fish too much.

3 Meanwhile, warm the naan breads to pack instructions, then serve with the curry.

CRISPY ONIONS
Add

Sprinkle 1 tablespoon crispy onions over the curry, for an extra **2 SmartPoints** per serving.

PILAU RICE
Side

SmartPoints to spare? You could serve this with pilau rice (p80) for an extra **4 SmartPoints** per serving.

SALMON WITH LENTILS & FETA

This is flavoured with za'atar – a spice mix you can find in most supermarkets.

Serves 4
PREP TIME 10 minutes
COOK TIME 15 minutes

Ingredients
4 x 130g skinless salmon fillets
2 x 400g tins green lentils, drained
  and rinsed
1 small cucumber, halved
  lengthways and sliced
125g pomegranate seeds
3 tablespoons pine nuts, toasted
75g light feta, crumbled
1 tablespoon chopped fresh dill
20g rocket
1 tablespoon extra virgin olive oil
Juice of 1 lemon
1 teaspoon za'atar

 SmartPoints
5 per serving

GF See page 6

Method
1 Preheat the oven to 200°C, fan 180°C, gas mark 6. Put the salmon on a large sheet of baking paper, then fold over the edges to form a parcel. Transfer to a baking sheet, then bake for 12-15 minutes. Set aside to cool then flake into large chunks.

2 Meanwhile, in a large bowl, combine the lentils with the cucumber, pomegranate seeds, pine nuts, feta, dill and rocket.

3 In a small jug, whisk together the oil, lemon juice and za'atar. Season and then drizzle over the lentil salad. Toss to combine, then stir through the salmon chunks.

 ## TOASTED PITTA
Toast 2 Weight Watchers pitta breads until really crisp, then break into pieces and toss through the salad, for an extra **2 SmartPoints** per serving.

 ## GREEK YOGURT
Top each portion with 1 tablespoon 0% fat natural Greek yogurt for no additional **SmartPoints**.

5 SEAFOOD SALADS

Fish works really well in salads – here are five flavoursome ideas to try.

TUNA LENTIL NICOISE
Serves 4

PREP TIME 10 minutes
COOK TIME 5 minutes

Boil 200g trimmed and halved **green beans** for 3 minutes until just tender. Drain and rinse under cold water to cool. Arrange the leaves from 1 **Cos lettuce** on a serving plate. Scatter over the beans, 250g ready-to-eat **lentils**, 300g quartered **baby plum tomatoes** and 1 thinly sliced **red onion**. Flake over 2 x 160g tins drained **tuna** in spring water. Whisk together 1 tablespoon **extra virgin olive oil**, the juice of 1 **lemon**, 1 tablespoon **white wine vinegar**, 1 teaspoon **wholegrain mustard**, 1 crushed **garlic clove** and 1 teaspoon clear **honey** and season to taste. Drizzle over the salad to serve.

SmartPoints
2 per serving **GF** See page 6

SUSHI-STYLE SALMON SALAD
Serves 4
PREP TIME 10 minutes **COOK TIME** 15 minutes

Preheat the oven to 200°C, fan 180°C, gas mark 6. Squeeze the juice of 1 **lime** over 4 skinless **salmon fillets**, then wrap them in a parcel of baking paper. Bake for 12-15 minutes, until cooked through. Leave to cool, then flake. Meanwhile, cook 2 x 250g packets **microwave basmati rice** to pack instructions. Whisk together ½ tablespoon **sesame oil**, 2 tablespoons **rice wine vinegar**, 1 teaspoon **wasabi paste** and 1 teaspoon **clear honey** to make a dressing. When the rice is cool, stir through the dressing, along with 50g chopped **rocket** and a handful of chopped **fresh chives**. Put the rice on a serving plate and top with the salmon, 1 **cucumber**, peeled into ribbons, and 60g **pickled ginger**. Serve with 4 tablespoons **soy sauce** in a dipping bowl.

7 SmartPoints
7 per serving **GF** See page 6

TROUT & BEETROOT SALAD
Serves 4
PREP TIME 10 minutes   **COOK TIME** 12-15 minutes

Preheat the oven to 200°C, fan 180°C, gas mark 6. Wrap 300g **trout fillets** in a parcel of baking paper. Bake for 12-15 minutes, until cooked through. Leave to cool, then flake, discarding the skin. Put 2 x 400g tins drained and rinsed **cannellini beans** in a large bowl. Whisk together 75g **0% fat natural Greek yogurt**, 1½ tablespoons **horseradish sauce** and the juice of ½ **lemon**, and season to taste. Mix half of the dressing through the beans. Mix the flaked trout with the beans and 250g cooked **beetroot**, cut into wedges. Serve the salad on the leaves of 2 **Little Gem lettuces**, with the remaining dressing on the side. You could use salmon, instead of trout, for no additional SmartPoints.

 **SmartPoints**
1 per serving   See page 6

ROASTED VEG & TUNA SALAD
Serves 4
PREP TIME 15 minutes   **COOK TIME** 30-35 minutes

Preheat the oven to 200°C, fan 180°C, gas mark 6. Cut 3 mixed **peppers** into chunks. Slice 3 **courgettes** into thick rounds and cut 2 **red onions** into wedges. Put the veg in a large roasting tray and drizzle over 1 tablespoon **rapeseed oil**. Roast for 30-35 minutes, until tender. Remove from the oven and set aside until it cools to room temperature, then mix through a 400g tin drained and rinsed **chickpeas**. In a small bowl, combine a handful of torn **fresh basil**, 1 crushed **garlic clove**, 1 tablespoon **extra virgin olive oil** and the juice of 1 **lemon**. Stir the mixture through the roasted veg to coat, then add 50g **young leaf spinach**. Season to taste. Transfer to a serving platter and top with 2 x 160g tins drained **tuna** in spring water, then serve.

 SmartPoints
3 per serving   See page 6

PRAWN, BROCCOLI & RICE NOODLE SALAD
Serves 4
PREP TIME 5 minutes   **COOK TIME** 10 minutes

Cook 250g **rice noodles** (use either regular or black ones) in boiling water for about 6 minutes, until cooked. Drain and rinse under cold water, then put into a bowl. Cook 200g **Tenderstem broccoli** for 3-4 minutes in a pan of boiling water until tender. Drain and refresh under cold water. Whisk together 1 tablespoon **sesame oil**, 2 tablespoons **soy sauce**, the juice of 2 **limes** and 1 teaspoon grated **fresh ginger**, then drizzle over the noodles and toss to coat. Divide between four bowls and top with the broccoli, a handful of **fresh coriander** and 300g **cooked king prawns**, then garnish with 2 finely sliced **spring onions** and serve.

8 SmartPoints value
SmartPoints
8 per serving

HONEY ROAST SALMON

This deliciously simple salmon dish is served with a haricot bean salad.

Serves 4
PREP TIME 10 minutes
COOK TIME 15 minutes

Ingredients
2 tablespoons clear honey
Juice of 2 lemons
1 teaspoon chilli flakes
Calorie controlled cooking spray
4 x 130g skinless salmon fillets
150g sugar snap peas, chopped
1 garlic clove
Handful fresh mint leaves
2 tablespoons extra virgin olive oil
2 x 400g tins haricot beans,
  drained and rinsed
40g rocket

 SmartPoints
4 per serving

GF See page 6

Method

1 Preheat the oven to 200°C, fan 180°C, gas mark 6. In a small bowl, combine the honey with half the lemon juice and the chilli flakes. Mist a non-stick baking sheet with cooking spray and put the salmon fillets on the sheet. Brush the honey mixture over the fish and bake for 15 minutes, basting halfway through with the juices.

2 Meanwhile, blanch the sugar snap peas for 1 minute in a pan of boiling water, then drain and refresh in cold water. Put half in a food processor with the garlic, mint, remaining lemon juice, olive oil and 1 tablespoon water. Blitz until you have a chunky dressing.

3 In a large serving bowl, toss together the haricot beans, rocket, remaining sugar snap peas and the dressing. Serve with the salmon.

 ## POTATO SALAD
If you have SmartPoints to spare, you can serve this with potato salad (p80), for an extra **4 SmartPoints** per serving.

 ## LEMON MAYO
This is also great served with lemon mayo (p79), for an extra **2 SmartPoints** per serving.

JAPANESE PRAWN & CABBAGE PANCAKES

These delicious prawn-filled pancakes are also known as Japanese pizza.

Makes 2
PREP TIME 10 minutes
COOK TIME 20 minutes

For the pancakes
4 eggs
60g plain flour
100ml vegetable stock, made with ½ stock cube
½ sweetheart cabbage, finely shredded
100g silken tofu, drained and roughly chopped
100g cooked and peeled prawns
4 spring onions, trimmed and thinly sliced
2 teaspoons rapeseed oil

To serve
2 teaspoons reduced-fat mayonnaise
2 teaspoons brown sauce
1 shallot, finely sliced
20g pickled ginger
1 teaspoon wasabi paste

 **SmartPoints** 6 per pancake

Method

1 Put the eggs in a large bowl and whisk lightly. Add the flour and continue to whisk until smooth, then add the stock and whisk again to incorporate. Stir the cabbage, tofu, prawns and spring onions into the mixture.

2 Heat half the oil in a 20cm non-stick frying pan over a medium heat, then spoon in half the mixture and smooth with a spatula. Cook for 4-5 minutes until the underside is golden brown, then flip over and cook for a further 2-3 minutes.

3 Transfer to a plate and keep warm while you cook the second pancake.

4 Serve the pancakes drizzled with the mayonnaise and brown sauce, and topped with the shallot, pickled ginger and wasabi paste.

 TOASTED SESAME SEEDS
Serve sprinkled with 1 teaspoon toasted sesame seeds per pancake, for an extra **1 SmartPoint** per serving.

 BACON
Add 2 bacon medallions to the top of each pancake before flipping for an extra **1 SmartPoint** per serving.

Fish & Seafood

SIDES

Try these easy accompaniments to your fish and seafood recipes…

Spicy chilli chips
+ 2 SmartPoints per serving

Tartare sauce
+ 1 SmartPoint per serving

Lemon mayo
+ 2 SmartPoints per serving

SPICY CHILLI CHIPS
Serves 4

PREP TIME 10 minutes
COOK TIME 40 minutes

Preheat the oven to 200°C, fan 180°C, gas mark 6. Peel and deseed 1 **butternut squash**, then cut into chunky chips and put in a large roasting tin. Mix together 1 teaspoon **garlic granules**, 1 teaspoon **cayenne pepper** and ½ teaspoon **chilli flakes**, then sprinkle over the chips and toss to coat. Drizzle over 1 tablespoon **rapeseed oil** and toss again. Bake for 35-40 minutes, or until golden and tender, then serve.

 SmartPoints
2 per serving

 See page 6

LEMON MAYO
Serves 4

PREP TIME 5 minutes

In a small bowl, mix together 75g reduced-fat **mayonnaise**, 100g 0% fat natural **Greek yogurt** and the grated zest and juice of 1 **lemon**. Season to taste and serve.

 SmartPoints
2 per serving

 See page 6

Potato salad
4 SmartPoints per serving

TARTARE SAUCE
Serves 4

PREP TIME 5 minutes

In a small bowl, mix together 150g **0% fat crème fraîche**, 1 teaspoon **Dijon mustard**, 2 small finely chopped **gherkins**, 1 tablespoon **capers** and 2 tablespoons finely chopped **fresh flat-leaf parsley**. Season to taste, then serve.

 SmartPoints
1 per serving

 See page 6

POTATO SALAD
Serves 4

PREP TIME 10 minutes
COOK TIME 10 minutes

Cook 500g small waxy **potatoes** in a pan of boiling water for 10 minutes until just cooked, then cool under running water and cut into chunks. Boil 2 **eggs** for 9 minutes, then cool under running water, peel and chop. Put the potatoes and eggs into a bowl with 4 thinly sliced **spring onions** and a handful of snipped **chives**. Mix together 6 tablespoons **0% fat natural Greek yogurt**, 3 tablespoons **reduced-fat mayonnaise** and 1 teaspoon **wholegrain mustard**, then stir into the salad. Season to taste, mix well to combine, then serve.

 SmartPoints
4 per serving

 See page 6

PILAU RICE
Serves 4

PREP TIME 5 minutes, plus standing
COOK TIME 25 minutes

Heat 1 tablespoon **rapeseed oil** in a large pan and fry 1 chopped **onion** for 6-8 minutes, until soft. Add 2 sliced **garlic cloves**, 1 teaspoon **cumin seeds**, 1 teaspoon ground **turmeric**, 1 pinch **ground cloves**, the crushed seeds of 4 **cardamom pods** and 1 **cinnamon stick**, and cook for 1-2 minutes. Add 275g **basmati rice** and stir well. Add 100g frozen **peas** and 550ml boiling water and bring to a boil. Reduce the heat to low, cover and simmer for 15 minutes. Remove from the heat and let stand for 10 minutes, then serve.

 SmartPoints
4 per serving

 See page 6

SQUASH & SWEET POTATO MASH
Serves 4

PREP TIME 10 minutes
COOK TIME 1 hour

Preheat the oven to 200°C, fan 180°C, gas mark 6. Halve 1 **butternut squash** lengthways, and scoop out the seeds. Halve 2 **sweet potatoes** lengthways and put in a roasting tin with the squash. Mist the veg with **calorie controlled cooking spray** and season to taste. Bake for 45 minutes-1 hour, until tender. Scoop out the flesh, discarding the skins. Mash together, season to taste and stir in 1 tablespoon half-fat **crème fraîche** and a handful of chopped **fresh coriander**, then serve.

 SmartPoints
3 per serving

 See page 6

Squash & sweet potato mash
+ 3 SmartPoints
per serving

Pilau rice
+ 4 SmartPoints
per serving

81

Chicken & turkey

CHICKEN CAPRESE

This classic Italian dish couldn't be more simple – or more delicious.

Serves 4
PREP TIME 15 minutes
COOK TIME 35 minutes

Ingredients
600g baby potatoes, halved
Calorie controlled cooking spray
Large handful fresh basil, leaves
  picked and roughly torn
2 teaspoons rapeseed oil
1 teaspoon red wine vinegar
1 shallot, finely chopped
4 skinless chicken breast fillets
500g plum tomatoes, sliced
225g light mozzarella, torn
2 teaspoons balsamic glaze

 SmartPoints
7 per serving

GF See page 6

Method

1 Preheat the oven to 190°C, fan 170°C, gas mark 5.
Put the potatoes in a large roasting tin, mist with
the cooking spray, then bake for 15 minutes.

2 Meanwhile, finely chop 1 tablespoon of the basil leaves
and mix together with 1 teaspoon of the oil, the red wine
vinegar and the shallot.

3 Put the chicken into the tin with the potatoes. Top each
chicken breast with 3 slices of tomato and spoon over the
basil and shallot mixture. Return to the oven and cook for
a further 20 minutes, until the potatoes are tender and
golden and the chicken is cooked through.

4 Combine the remaining tomatoes, basil and rapeseed oil
with the mozzarella and season to taste. Serve with the
potatoes and chicken, drizzled with the balsamic glaze.

 ## HASSELBACK POTATOES
Instead of the baby potatoes, try serving this
with mini hasselback potatoes (p109), for
a total of **9 SmartPoints** per serving.

 ## OLIVES
Scatter 25g sliced black olives over the
chicken when serving for an extra
1 SmartPoint per serving.

GOLDEN CHICKEN

Serve this honey and mustard chicken with a simple butterbean houmous.

Serves 4

PREP TIME 10 minutes, plus marinating and resting
COOK TIME 15 minutes

Ingredients

500g skinless chicken breast fillets, flattened to 1cm in thickness
2 teaspoons clear honey
1 tablespoon wholegrain mustard, plus an extra ½ teaspoon
½ teaspoon ground turmeric
1 teaspoon olive oil
250g frozen peas
400g tin butterbeans, drained and rinsed
50g pea shoots
Juice of 1 lemon

 SmartPoints
2 per serving

 See page 6

Method

1 Put the chicken, honey, 1 tablespoon mustard, the turmeric and olive oil into a bowl and mix together. Leave to marinate for 10 minutes.

2 Heat a griddle pan over a medium heat. In batches, griddle the chicken for 5 minutes on each side, until golden and cooked through. Leave to rest for 5 minutes.

3 Bring a small pan of water to the boil, add the peas and cook for 3 minutes, then drain. Run under cold water to cool, then mix with half the butterbeans and the pea shoots in a serving bowl.

4 Mash the remaining butterbeans in a small bowl and mix in the lemon juice, extra ½ teaspoon mustard and any cooking juices from the chicken. Slice the chicken and serve with the salad and butterbean houmous.

Add | ## ALMONDS
Scatter 25g of flaked or chopped whole almonds over the chicken when serving for an extra **5 SmartPoints** per serving.

Side | ## LEMON & HERB BULGUR WHEAT
You could serve this with a side dish of lemon & herb bulgur wheat (p110), for an extra **3 SmartPoints** per serving.

CHICKEN ENCHILADAS

Mexican-style wraps baked in a tomato sauce and topped with cheese.

Serves 4
PREP TIME 20 minutes
COOK TIME 35 minutes

Ingredients
Calorie controlled cooking spray
300g skinless chicken breast
  fillets, sliced
1 small onion, sliced
1 red pepper, deseeded and sliced
1 garlic clove, finely chopped
½ teaspoon ground cumin
198g tin sweetcorn, drained
215g tin kidney beans, drained
  and gently crushed
300g passata
2 tablespoons fresh coriander,
  chopped, plus extra for garnish
4 large wholemeal wraps
100g reduced-fat soured cream
25g grated mozzarella cheese

 SmartPoints
7 per serving

Method

1 Mist a large frying pan with the cooking spray and cook the chicken slices over a high heat for 5 minutes, turning, until golden.

2 Add the onion and pepper. Cook for 5 minutes, adding the garlic and cumin for the last minute. Stir in the sweetcorn, crushed beans and 200g of the passata and bring to a gentle simmer. Cook for 1 minute, then stir in the chopped coriander.

3 Preheat the oven to 200°C, fan 180°C, gas mark 6. Divide the chicken mixture between the wraps and roll up tightly. Place them seam side down into a rectangular baking dish, misted with cooking spray. Mix the remaining passata with the soured cream and pour over the top. Scatter over the cheese and bake for 15-20 minutes, until golden. Serve topped with the extra coriander.

 ## CHORIZO
Fry 50g sliced chorizo after the chicken in step 1 until it starts to turn crisp, then add it to the top of the enchiladas before sprinkling with the cheese, for an extra **2 SmartPoints** per serving.

 ## GUACAMOLE
Try serving this with a side dish of guacamole (p110) for an extra **5 SmartPoints** per serving.

4 QUICK COOKED CHICKEN BREAST IDEAS

Fancy an easy lunch? Use cooked chicken breast fillets
for these tasty ideas.

TOASTED CHICKEN SANDWICH
Makes 1
PREP TIME 5 minutes **COOK TIME** 5 minutes

Mix 60g **quark** with a small handful of chopped
fresh **chives**, then season to taste. Toast 1 brown
sandwich thin and spread over the chive quark.
Top with 1 shredded cooked **skinless chicken
breast fillet**, a small handful of **rocket** and the
other half of the thin, then serve.

 SmartPoints
4 per sandwich

CHICKEN & GRAPE SALAD
Serves 4
PREP TIME 10 minutes

Toss together 160g mixed **salad leaves** with
250g black and green **grapes**, halved, and
1 small sliced **cucumber**. Whisk together
1 tablespoon **extra virgin olive oil** with the juice
of 1 **lemon**, 2 finely chopped sprigs of **rosemary**
and 1 crushed **garlic clove**. Season to taste,
then drizzle over the salad and toss to dress. Add
4 sliced cooked **skinless chicken breast fillets**
and toss to combine. Divide among 4 bowls
and garnish with 50g **almonds**.

 SmartPoints
4 per serving GF See page 6

POTATO, SPINACH & CHICKEN SALAD
Serves 4
PREP TIME 10 minutes **COOK TIME** 35 minutes

Preheat the oven to 200°C, fan 180°C, gas mark
6. Cut 500g baby new **potatoes** in half and put
in a roasting tin. Drizzle with ½ tablespoon **olive
oil** and season. Roast for 30-35 minutes, or until
tender. Leave to cool, then put in a bowl with 160g
young leaf spinach, 150g halved **cherry tomatoes**
and 4 shredded cooked **skinless chicken breast
fillets**. Whisk together 1 tablespoon **extra virgin
olive oil**, the juice of 1 **lemon**, 1 teaspoon
wholegrain mustard and 1 teaspoon **clear honey**.
Drizzle over the salad and toss to combine.

 SmartPoints
5 per serving GF See page 6

CHICKEN WITH PESTO PASTA
Serves 4
PREP TIME 10 minutes **COOK TIME** 15 minutes

Cook 250g **wholewheat pasta** to pack instructions.
Drain, reserving the pasta water, then return the
pasta to the pan. Add 100g **low-fat soft cheese**,
2 tablespoons **pesto** and a ladleful of the pasta
water. Stir until the cheese melts and the pasta
is coated. Toss through 4 diced cooked **skinless
chicken breast fillets**, 150g **young leaf spinach**
and a handful of chopped **fresh basil** until the
spinach has wilted. Season to taste, then serve.

 SmartPoints
8 per serving

TURKEY-STUFFED ROASTED SQUASH

Sweet butternut squash filled with a spicy mix of turkey, beans and tomatoes.

Serves 4
PREP TIME 15 minutes
COOK TIME 55 minutes

Ingredients

2 x 900g butternut squash,
  halved and deseeded
Calorie controlled cooking spray
300g 2% fat turkey breast mince
6 spring onions, sliced
1 garlic clove, finely chopped
1 teaspoon ground cumin
1 tablespoon chipotle paste
400g tin chopped tomatoes
400g tin black beans, drained
  and rinsed
Small handful fresh coriander,
  chopped, plus extra coriander
  leaves, to serve

0 SmartPoints
0 per serving

GF See page 6

Method

1 Preheat the oven to 200°C, fan 180°C, gas mark 6.
  Put the butternut squash halves on a large baking tray,
  cut side up. Roast for 45 minutes, until tender.

2 Meanwhile, mist a large non-stick frying pan with cooking
  spray and put over a medium-high heat. Add the turkey
  mince and cook for 5 minutes, stirring to break up any
  lumps. Add the spring onions and garlic and cook for
  3 minutes. Stir in the cumin, chipotle paste, tomatoes and
  beans and bring to a gentle simmer. Cook for 2-3 minutes,
  then add the coriander and season to taste.

3 Spoon the turkey mixture into the butternut squash halves
  and roast for a further 10 minutes. Serve garnished with
  the extra coriander.

FETA
Sprinkle 50g crumbled light feta over the
top of the turkey mixture before returning
the squash to the oven for an extra
3 SmartPoints per serving.

SOURED CREAM
Serve with 1 tablespoon reduced-fat
soured cream per person for an extra
1 SmartPoint per serving.

CHICKEN TIKKA CHAPATI WRAPS

Spicy chicken skewers served in warm flatbreads with loads of fresh tomatoes.

Serves 4
PREP TIME 20 minutes,
plus marinating
COOK TIME 20 minutes

For the marinade
100g 0% fat natural yogurt
1 garlic clove, chopped
½ green chilli, deseeded
  and chopped
1cm-piece fresh ginger, grated
½ teaspoon ground cumin
1 teaspoon ground coriander
½ teaspoon tikka curry powder
500g skinless chicken breast fillets,
  cut into bite-size chunks

For the wraps
400g tomatoes, roughly chopped
½ small red onion, thinly sliced
Pared zest and juice of ½ lemon
2 tablespoons chopped fresh
  coriander, plus extra to garnish
4 sprigs fresh mint, leaves picked
  and chopped
4 chapati wraps
4 tablespoons 0% fat natural
  yogurt, to serve

SmartPoints
8 per serving

Method

1 To make the marinade, put all the marinade ingredients, except the chicken, into a small food processor and blitz until smooth. Pour into a bowl with the chicken and leave to marinate, covered, for 30 minutes.

2 Combine the tomatoes, onion, lemon zest and juice, coriander and mint in a bowl and season to taste.

3 Preheat the grill to medium-high. Thread the chicken pieces onto skewers, discarding any leftover marinade, and cook under the grill for 15-20 minutes, turning every 5 minutes, until golden and cooked through.

4 Put the chapati wraps onto a baking sheet and warm under the grill for 1 minute on each side. Serve the chapatis with the chicken tikka pieces and salad, drizzled with the yogurt and topped with the extra coriander.

ALMONDS
Sprinkle over 25g flaked or chopped almonds for an extra **1 SmartPoint** per serving

MANGO CHUTNEY
Try serving this with mango chutney (p109), for an extra **3 SmartPoints** per serving.

TURKEY & MUSHROOM LASAGNE

This pasta-free turkey lasagne is full of flavour, but low in SmartPoints.

Serves 4
PREP TIME 25 minutes
COOK TIME 35 minutes

Ingredients
1 butternut squash, peeled, deseeded and thinly sliced
Calorie controlled cooking spray
1 tablespoon rapeseed oil
1 onion, finely chopped
1 carrot, finely chopped
1 stick celery, finely chopped
400g 2% fat turkey breast mince
½ tablespoon tomato purée
2 x 400g tins chopped tomatoes with onion and garlic
100g dried green lentils
Small handful fresh basil, leaves picked and torn
6 sprigs fresh thyme, leaves picked and roughly chopped
200g baby button chestnut mushrooms, sliced
100g natural cottage cheese
20g Parmesan cheese, finely grated
1 egg yolk

 SmartPoints
3 per serving

  See page 6

Method
1 Preheat the oven to 200°C, fan 180°C, gas mark 6. Put the butternut squash slices onto non-stick baking sheets and mist with cooking spray. Season to taste, then bake for 20 minutes, until just tender.

2 Meanwhile, heat the oil in a large pan over a medium heat. Add the onion, carrot and celery and cook for 5 minutes. Add the turkey mince, turn up the heat and cook for 5 minutes, stirring. Add the tomato purée, tomatoes, lentils, basil, thyme and 400ml water, bring to a simmer, cover and cook for 15 minutes. Add the mushrooms and cook for a further 10 minutes.

3 Whizz the cottage cheese, 15g of the Parmesan and the egg yolk in a mini food processor, until smooth.

4 Put half the turkey mince mixture into the bottom of a rectangular baking dish and top with half the butternut squash slices. Spoon over the remaining turkey mince mixture and arrange the rest of the butternut squash slices on top. Spoon the cottage cheese mixture on last, scatter over the remaining Parmesan and bake for 15 minutes, until golden.

 ## GARLIC BREAD
Serve with ¼ ready-made reduced-fat garlic and herb baguette, for an extra **4 SmartPoints** per serving.

 ## PASTA
If you fancy pasta with this, chop the dish up into small pieces and serve with 240g wholewheat spaghetti, cooked to pack instructions for an extra **6 SmartPoints** per serving.

STICKY PEANUT BUTTER CHICKEN

This super-quick chicken and noodle dish is packed with Asian-style flavours.

Serves 4
PREP TIME 10 minutes
COOK TIME 15 minutes

Ingredients
500g skinless chicken breast fillets
150g wholewheat noodles
4 spring onions, shredded
1 carrot, peeled and sliced
  into ribbons
50g young leaf spinach, shredded

For the sauce
3 tablespoons peanut butter
1 tablespoon soy sauce
1 teaspoon clear honey
Juice of 1 lime
1 red chilli, deseeded and
  finely chopped
1cm-piece fresh ginger,
  peeled and grated
Handful fresh coriander,
  roughly chopped

SmartPoints
9 per serving

Method

1 Bring a pan of water to the boil. Reduce to a simmer, add the chicken, then cover and poach for 10 minutes. Remove with a slotted spoon and leave to cool slightly, then shred. Put the noodles into the same water and cook for 5 minutes, or to pack instructions. Drain and set aside.

2 Meanwhile, make the sauce. Combine the peanut butter, soy sauce, honey, lime juice, chilli, ginger and 6 tablespoons of boiling water in a pan. Bring to a simmer, then remove from the heat and stir in the chicken and half the coriander.

3 Divide the noodles between bowls. Top with the spring onions, carrot, spinach, the remaining coriander leaves and finally, the chicken.

PEANUTS
Scatter over 25g chopped unsalted roasted peanuts when serving for an extra **4 SmartPoints** per serving.

PEA & CORIANDER RICE
Instead of the noodles, you could serve this with pea & coriander rice (p110) for an extra **4 SmartPoints** per serving.

5 CHICKEN BAKES

These one-pot bakes take just a few minutes to prepare.

GARLIC & HERB CHICKEN

Serves 4

PREP TIME 5 minutes   **COOK TIME** 55 minutes

Preheat the oven to 200°C, fan 180°C, gas mark 6. Put 800g halved new **potatoes**, 6 skin-on **garlic cloves** and a few sprigs of **fresh rosemary** and **fresh thyme** into a roasting tin. Toss together with 1 tablespoon **rapeseed oil** and season to taste. Cover with foil and bake for 30 minutes. Add 4 **skinless chicken breast fillets** and cook, uncovered, for another 20-25 minutes, until cooked through and golden. Add 1 **lemon**, cut into wedges, to the tin, squeezing over some of the juice, then serve.

 SmartPoints
5 per servin **GF** See page 6

MARMALADE CHICKEN
Serves 4
PREP TIME 15 minutes   **COOK TIME** 1 hour 5 minutes

Preheat the oven to 200°C, fan 180°C, gas mark 6. Trim, peel and cut 500g raw **beetroot** into thin wedges, then put into a large roasting tin with 2 chopped **carrots**, 2 chopped **parnsips** and 1 sliced **onion**. Mix together 1 tablespoon **rapeseed oil**, the grated zest of ½ an **orange**, 2 tablespoons **marmalade**, the juice of 1 **lemon** and 1 teaspoon mild **chilli powder**, then drizzle it over the vegetables. Season, cover with foil and bake for 35-40 minutes. Add 4 **skinless chicken breast fillets** to the tin and bake, uncovered for another 20-25 minutes, until golden and sticky. Serve scattered with 2 tablespoons chopped **fresh flat-leaf parsley**.

6 SmartPoints value

SmartPoints
6 per serving   **GF** See page 6

INDIAN-STYLE CHICKEN
Serves 4
PREP TIME 15 minutes   **COOK TIME** 55 minutes

Preheat the oven to 200°C, fan 180°C, gas mark 6. Put 600g chopped waxy **potatoes**, 1 **cauliflower**, cut into florets, 200g **cherry tomatoes**, halved, and 1 **onion**, cut into wedges, into a large roasting tin. Mist with **calorie controlled cooking spray** and toss together with 1 teaspoon **ground cumin**, 1 teaspoon **ground coriander** and 2 teaspoons **garam masala**, then season to taste. Cover with foil and bake for 35 minutes. Add 4 **skinless chicken breast fillets** to the tin and bake, uncovered, for another 20-25 minutes. Stir through 100g **young leaf spinach**. Meanwhile, mix 100g **0% fat natural yogurt** with half a finely chopped **garlic clove**, a small handful of chopped **fresh mint** and 1 tablespoon **lemon juice**. Serve the traybake with the dressing drizzled over.

 **SmartPoints**
4 per serving See page 6

CHICKEN, CHORIZO & BROCCOLI
Serves 4
PREP TIME 10 minutes   **COOK TIME** 1 hour

Preheat the oven to 200°C, fan 180°C, gas mark 6. Put 800g halved new **potatoes**, 2 small **red onions**, cut into wedges, 4 unpeeled **garlic cloves** that have been lightly crushed, and the chopped leaves from 2 sprigs of **fresh rosemary** into a roasting tin. Toss together with 1 tablespoon **rapeseed oil** and season to taste. Cover with foil and bake for 30 minutes. Add 100g sliced **chorizo**, 1 head of **broccoli**, cut into florets, and 4 **skinless chicken breast fillets** to the tin and cook, uncovered, for another 20-25 minutes, until cooked through and golden.

 SmartPoints
9 per serving See page 6

MEXICAN-STYLE CHICKEN
Serves 4
PREP TIME 10 minutes   **COOK TIME** 55 minutes

Preheat the oven to 200°C, fan 180°C, gas mark 6. Put 2 peeled and thickly-sliced **sweet potatoes**, 1 sliced red and 1 sliced green **pepper**, 1 sliced **red onion**, 4 unpeeled lightly crushed **garlic cloves** and 3 sliced **tomatoes** into a large baking dish. Season to taste. Cover with foil and bake for 30 minutes. Combine 4 **skinless chicken breast fillets** with 1 tablespoon **rapeseed oil**, 1 teaspoon **dried oregano**, 2 teaspoons **smoked paprika** and 1 tablespoon **red wine vinegar**. Add to the tin, pour over any remaining marinade and bake, uncovered, for 20-25 minutes. Scatter over 2 tablespoons chopped **fresh coriander** and serve with **lime** wedges.

4 SmartPoints value

SmartPoints
4 per serving   ○ **GF** See page 6

ASIAN-STYLE TURKEY MEATBALLS

This quick, easy and colourful stir-fry will be a hit with all the family.

Serves 4
PREP TIME 10 minutes
COOK TIME 15 minutes

Ingredients
500g 2% fat turkey breast mince
4 spring onions, finely chopped
1 garlic clove, finely chopped
1 red chilli, deseeded and
    finely chopped
1 teaspoon clear honey
Small handful fresh coriander,
    chopped, plus extra to serve
3 tablespoons soy sauce
1 teaspoon sesame oil
Calorie controlled cooking spray
325g mixed vegetable stir-fry pack
100g baby corn, halved lengthways
100g mangetout
180g wholewheat noodles

 SmartPoints
6 per serving

Method

1 Preheat the grill to medium-high. Put the turkey mince in a bowl with the spring onions, garlic, chilli, honey, two-thirds of the coriander, 1 tablespoon of the soy sauce and ½ teaspoon of the sesame oil. Mix, then shape into 12 balls.

2 Put the meatballs onto a foil-lined baking sheet. Cook under the grill for 15 minutes, turning once, until golden and cooked through. The meatballs can be made ahead of time and frozen.

3 Meanwhile, mist a frying pan with cooking spray. Put over a high heat and stir-fry the mixed vegetables, baby corn and mangetout for 5 minutes. Add 1 tablespoon of the soy sauce and the remaining sesame oil and coriander.

4 Bring a pan of water to the boil and cook the noodles for 5 minutes, or to pack instructions. Drain.

5 Serve the noodles topped with the stir-fried veg and meatballs. Drizzle over the remaining soy sauce and garnish with the extra coriander.

 ## SESAME & CHILLI NOODLES
Instead of the plain noodles, spice up this dish with sesame & chilli noodles (p110) for no additional **SmartPoints** per serving.

 ## CASHEW NUTS
Sprinkle 40g roughly chopped cashew nuts over the stir-fry when serving for an extra **2 SmartPoints** per serving.

TURKISH-STYLE PIZZAS

Spiced turkey mince makes a tasty topping for these shortcut pizzas.

Serves 4
PREP TIME 15 minutes
COOK TIME 20 minutes

Ingredients
Calorie controlled cooking spray
400g 2% fat turkey breast mince
4 spring onions, sliced
1 garlic clove, finely chopped
½ red or orange pepper, deseeded
  and diced
2 tomatoes, roughly chopped
½ teaspoon each paprika, ground
  cumin and ground coriander
2 tablespoon chopped fresh mint
4 small folded flatbreads
75g 0% fat natural yogurt
1 teaspoon tahini
½ teaspoon sumac (optional)
40g pomegranate seeds

 SmartPoints
3 per serving

Method

1 Preheat the oven to 200°C, fan 180°C, gas mark 6. Mist a pan with cooking spray, put over a high heat and cook the turkey for 5 minutes. Add the spring onions, garlic, pepper, tomatoes and spices and cook for a further 5 minutes. Stir in half the mint and season to taste.

2 Gently unfold the flatbreads and put onto a baking sheet. Top with the mince mixture and bake for 10 minutes.

3 Meanwhile, in a small bowl, mix together the yogurt, tahini, sumac (if using) and half the remaining mint. Serve the pizzas topped with the pomegranate seeds, tahini sauce and remaining mint.

 **FETA**
Scatter 50g crumbled light feta cheese over the pizzas before cooking for an extra **3 SmartPoints** per serving.

 LEMON YOGURT DRESSING
This is great served drizzled with lemon yogurt dressing (p110) for no additional **SmartPoints** per serving.

Mango chutney
+ 3 SmartPoints
per serving

Guacamole
+ 5 SmartPoints
per serving

Mini hasselback potatoes
+ 5 SmartPoints
per serving

Chicken & turkey

SIDES

Make mealtimes extra special with these side dishes that go perfectly with chicken or turkey.

Lemon yogurt dressing
+ 0 SmartPoints per serving

MINI HASSELBACK POTATOES

Serves 4

PREP TIME 5 minutes
COOK TIME 30 minutes

Preheat the oven to 200°C, fan 180°C, gas mark 6. Thinly slice 800g baby **potatoes** ¾ of the way down into each potato, taking care not to slice all the way through. Put in a large roasting tin and toss with ½ tablespoon **rapeseed oil** and ½ teaspoon **dried oregano**. Season to taste, then roast for 25-30 minutes, until tender and golden.

 SmartPoints
5 per serving

  See page 6

MANGO CHUTNEY

Serves 8

PREP TIME 10 minutes
COOK TIME 35 minutes

Put 200ml **white wine vinegar** into a pan with 2 chopped **garlic cloves**, 25g **caster sugar**, 100g chopped pitted **Medjool dates**, ½ a peeled and grated **cooking apple**, 200g chopped **mango** flesh and 20g grated **fresh ginger**. Cook over a low heat until the sugar has dissolved, then simmer, partially covered, for 30 minutes, until the mango is tender and the chutney has reduced and thickened. If not using straight away, spoon into sterilised jars – it will keep for up to 4 weeks in the fridge.

 SmartPoints
3 per serving

  See page 6

GUACAMOLE
Serves 4
PREP TIME 10 minutes

Mash the flesh from 2 **avocados**, then mix with 1 deseeded and finely chopped **green chilli**, 3 finely chopped **spring onions**, 1 diced **tomato** and 2 tablespoons chopped **fresh coriander**. Stir in the juice of ½ **lime**, season to taste, then serve.

 SmartPoints
5 per serving

 See page 6

LEMON YOGURT DRESSING
Serves 4
PREP TIME 5 minutes

Mix together 100g **0% fat natural yogurt**, the zest and juice of ½ **lemon**, ½ finely chopped **garlic clove**, ¼ teaspoon **ground cumin** and ½ tablespoon chopped fresh **mint**, then serve.

 SmartPoints
0 per serving

 See page 6

LEMON & HERB BULGUR WHEAT
Serves 4
PREP TIME 5 minutes
COOK TIME 15 minutes

Bring a pan of water to the boil. Cook 150g **bulgur wheat** for 12-15 minutes or until tender, then drain. Stir in the zest and juice of 1 **lemon**, 2 tablespoons chopped **fresh parsley**, 1 tablespoon chopped **fresh coriander** and ½ tablespoon chopped **fresh mint**. Serve with lemon wedges.

SmartPoints
3 per serving

SESAME & CHILLI NOODLES
Serves 4
PREP TIME 5 minutes
COOK TIME 5 minutes

Bring a pan of water to the boil. Cook 150g **wholewheat noodles** for 5 minutes, to pack instructions, then drain, reserving 1 tablespoon of the cooking water. Stir in 2 teaspoons **chilli sauce**, the juice of 1 **lime**, 1 teaspoon **sesame oil**, 3 sliced **spring onions**, 1 teaspoon **toasted sesame seeds**, and the reserved cooking water, then serve.

 SmartPoints
5 per serving

PEA & CORIANDER RICE
Serves 4
PREP TIME 5 minutes
COOK TIME 35 minutes

Bring a large pan of water to the boil, add 150g **brown rice** and cook for 25-30 minutes, until tender, adding 200g **frozen peas** for the last 3 minutes of cooking time. Drain and stir together with 3 tablespoons chopped **fresh coriander** and 2 finely sliced **spring onions**.

 SmartPoints
4 per serving

  See page 6

Pea & coriander rice
4 SmartPoints
per serving

Lemon & herb bulgur wheat
3 SmartPoints
per serving

Sesame & chilli noodles
5 SmartPoints
per serving

Meat

CHILLI BEEF WITH HOUMOUS

Sirloin steaks are served with houmous and a tomato and pitta bread salad.

Serves 4

PREP TIME 20 minutes
COOK TIME 25 minutes

Ingredients

2 wholemeal pitta breads
Calorie controlled cooking spray
350g cherry tomatoes, halved
1 small red onion, thinly sliced
2 tablespoons fresh flat-leaf parsley,
  finely chopped
1 tablespoon red wine vinegar
4 thin sirloin steaks, fat trimmed
1½ teaspoons chilli flakes

For the houmous

3 garlic cloves
Juice of 1 lemon
½ teaspoon salt
2 x 400g tins chickpeas, drained
  and rinsed
50g tahini
½ teaspoon ground cumin

SmartPoints
10 per serving

Method

1 Preheat the oven to 190°C, fan 170°C, gas mark 5. Cut each pitta bread into quarters, then cut each quarter in half to make a total of 16 triangles. Arrange them in a single layer on a large baking sheet and mist with cooking spray. Season to taste and toss to coat. Bake for 20 minutes, turning once, until crisp and golden.

2 Meanwhile, make the houmous. Put the garlic, lemon juice and salt into a food processor and pulse until the garlic is roughly chopped. Add the chickpeas, tahini and cumin and process, gradually adding 150ml ice-cold water until the houmous is smooth and thick. For a thinner consistency, add a little more water. Transfer the houmous to a pan and gently warm through.

3 Toss together the tomatoes, onion, parsley, vinegar and pitta chips in a serving bowl, then season to taste and set aside.

4 Rub the steaks with the chilli flakes and season to taste. Mist a griddle pan with cooking spray and put over a high heat. Griddle the steaks for 2 minutes on each side, or until cooked to your liking. Serve with the houmous and tomato salad.

 ### EXTRA VIRGIN OLIVE OIL

Drizzle 1 tablespoon extra virgin olive oil over the tomato salad for an extra **1 SmartPoint** per serving.

 ### CARROT & HARISSA HOUMOUS

Instead of the plain houmous, you could also serve this with carrot & harissa houmous (p138), for an extra **1 SmartPoint** per serving.

BEEF & MUSHROOM STEW

A warming, flavour-packed stew that's just right for chilly evenings.

Serves 4
PREP TIME 20 minutes
COOK TIME 2 hours 35 minutes

Ingredients
800g extra-lean diced
  casserole steak
Calorie controlled cooking spray
8 shallots, peeled
3 sticks celery, roughly chopped
2 carrots, peeled and
  cut into large chunks
600ml rich beef stock made
  with one beef stock pot
1 sprig fresh rosemary
1 tablespoon plain flour
250g button mushrooms
1 tablespoon redcurrant jelly
2 garlic cloves, finely chopped
3 x 400g tins butterbeans,
  drained and rinsed
225ml semi-skimmed milk
1 tablespoon fresh thyme leaves
Small handful fresh flat-leaf parsley,
  roughly chopped

SmartPoints
8 per serving

Method

1 Season the meat to taste. Mist a large flameproof casserole with cooking spray and set over a medium-high heat. Fry the beef in batches until browned all over, then set aside.

2 Mist the casserole with cooking spray again and cook the shallots, celery and carrots for 10 minutes, or until just softened.

3 Return the steak to the pot, then add the stock and the rosemary. Bring to the boil, then reduce the heat to low, cover and simmer for approximately 2 hours, or until the meat is tender.

4 Blend the flour with 1 tablespoon water and add to the casserole, along with the button mushrooms and the redcurrant jelly. Cook, uncovered, for 15 minutes until the stew has thickened and the mushrooms are tender.

5 Meanwhile, mist a large frying pan with cooking spray. Fry the garlic for 1 minute, then add the beans and cook for 5 minutes, until the beans are warmed through. Add the milk, then mash over a low heat. Season to taste, then stir through the thyme. Serve the mash with the stew, topped with the chopped parsley. The stew can be frozen for up to 2 months.

ALE
For a deeper flavour, replace 250ml of the stock with real ale, for a total of **9 SmartPoints** per serving.

HORSERADISH SAUCE
Stir 2 tablespoons horseradish sauce through the stew before serving for an extra **1 SmartPoint** per serving.

4 QUICK SLICED HAM IDEAS

Ready-cooked ham is a great standby ingredient for quick brunches and lunches.

SPINACH, HAM & EGG MUFFINS
Makes 12
PREP TIME 10 minutes

Preheat the oven to 180°C, fan 160°C, gas mark 4. Put 100g **young leaf spinach** in a microwave-safe bowl, cover and cook on high for 2 minutes. Squeeze out excess moisture and chop. Mist a 12-hole muffin tin with **calorie controlled cooking spray**. In a bowl, whisk together 10 **eggs** with 115ml **semi-skimmed milk**. Stir in 50g grated **light mature Cheddar**, 50g chopped **wafer thin ham** and the spinach. Spoon the mixture into the muffin tin and bake for 25 minutes until golden.

 SmartPoints
1 per muffin   See page 6

PEA, MINT & HAM SOUP
Serves 4
PREP TIME 10 minutes **COOK TIME** 15 minutes

Put 800ml **chicken stock**, 1 finely chopped **onion**, 1 chopped **potato** and 450g frozen **peas** in a medium pan. Bring to the boil, then reduce the heat and simmer for 10 minutes or until the potato is tender. Stir in 2 tablespoons chopped **fresh mint** and use a stick blender to process until smooth, reserving some of the peas before blending. Stir in 125g chopped **wafer thin ham**, reserving some, and heat through. Serve garnished with the reserved peas and ham.

 **SmartPoints**
2 per serving  See page 6

HAM & WALDORF TARTINE
Serves 1
PREP TIME 5 minutes

Toast 1 **sandwich thin** and top with 2 slices **wafer thin ham**. Cut a quarter of an **apple** and half a **celery stick** into matchsticks, and mix with ¼ teaspoon **white wine vinegar** and 1 tablespoon **fat-free fromage frais**. Pile on top of the ham and scatter with snipped fresh **chives**, then serve.

 **SmartPoints**
5 per serving

HAM & LEEK RISOTTO
Serves 4
PREP TIME 15 minutes **COOK TIME** 40 minutes

Spray a pan with **calorie controlled cooking spray** and put over a medium heat. Add 2 sliced **leeks** and cook for 3-4 minutes until soft. Add 2 chopped **garlic cloves** and 225g **Arborio rice** and cook for 1 minute. Add 900ml **chicken stock**, made with 2 stock cubes, a little at a time, stirring until the liquid has been absorbed by the rice, then add more stock. Repeat until all the stock has been used and the rice is tender – about 25-30 minutes. Stir in 100g shredded **wafer thin ham** until warmed through. Remove from the heat and stir in 30g grated **Parmesan**, reserving some to garnish. Season to taste and served sprinkled with the reserved Parmesan.

 SmartPoints
8 per serving  See page 6

Meat

SAUSAGE & SWEET POTATO BAKE

Once you've done the preparation, this tasty one-tray dish looks after itself.

Serves 4
PREP TIME 15 minutes
COOK TIME 45 minutes

Ingredients

8 reduced-fat pork sausages
2 sweet potatoes, peeled and cut
 into thin wedges
2 red onions, cut into wedges
1 red pepper, deseeded and cut
 into strips
1 yellow pepper, deseeded and
 cut into strips
4 garlic cloves
1 tablespoon wholegrain mustard
½ teaspoon smoked paprika
Calorie controlled cooking spray
220g cherry tomatoes

 **SmartPoints**
6 per serving

Method

1 Preheat the oven to 200°C, fan 180°C, gas mark 6.
 Put the sausages, sweet potatoes, onions, peppers
 and garlic in a large bowl.

2 Add the mustard and paprika, then mist everything with
 cooking spray and mix together with your hands until
 everything is coated.

3 Spread out the sausages and vegetables in a large
 roasting tin and bake for 30 minutes. Add the tomatoes
 to the tin and bake for a further 15 minutes or until the
 sweet potatoes are cooked through.

 ## SOURED CREAM
Serve each portion topped with 1 tablespoon
reduced-fat soured cream for an extra
1 SmartPoint per serving.

 ## GARLIC CROUTONS
For extra crunch, serve this with garlic croutons
(p137) for an extra **3 SmartPoints** per serving.

PORK & FENNEL RAGU

Keep the SmartPoints low by serving this with butternut squash noodles.

Serves 4

PREP TIME 5 minutes
COOK TIME 30 minutes

Ingredients

Calorie controlled cooking spray
1 onion, finely chopped
2 garlic cloves, finely chopped
1 tablespoon fennel seeds
½ teaspoon chilli flakes
500g 5% fat pork mince
500g passata
1 teaspoon caster sugar
2 x 300g packs prepared butternut
  squash noodles
Grated zest of 1 lemon
Small handful fresh flat-leaf parsley,
  roughly chopped

 SmartPoints
4 per serving

 See page 6

Method

1 Mist a large deep frying pan with cooking spray and put over a medium-high heat. Cook the onion for 6-8 minutes until softened, then add the garlic, fennel seeds and chilli flakes and cook for 1 minute.

2 Add the pork and cook until browned all over, breaking up any lumps using the back of a wooden spoon. Stir in the passata and sugar, and simmer for 15 minutes until thickened slightly.

3 Meanwhile, cook the butternut noodles to pack instructions, then add to the pan with the ragú, season to taste and toss to combine. Serve topped with the lemon zest and parsley.

 ## PASTA
Instead of the butternut squash noodles, cook 240g wholewheat pasta and serve with the ragù for a total of **10 SmartPoints** per serving.

 ## PARMESAN
Serve this with 60g grated Parmesan to sprinkle over for an extra **2 SmartPoints** per serving.

 ## TOMATO & RED ONION SALAD
Try serving this with tomato & red onion salad (p138) for an extra **3 SmartPoints** per serving.

5 BRILLIANT BURGERS

Fancy a Friday night fakeaway? Try one of these easy ideas.

CLASSIC BEEF BURGER

Makes 4

PREP TIME 10 minutes   **COOK TIME** 15 minutes

In a small bowl, mix ½ finely chopped **onion**, 500g **5% fat beef mince** and 1 lightly beaten **egg** until combined. Shape the mixture into 4 patties about 2cm thick. Mist a griddle pan or frying pan with **calorie controlled cooking spray** and put over a medium heat. Cook the burgers for 15 minutes, turning occasionally, until cooked through. Serve each burger in a small **burger bun** with **lettuce** leaves and sliced **red onion**, **gherkin** and **tomato**.

8 SmartPoints value

SmartPoints
8 per burger

BLUE CHEESE BURGER

Makes 4

PREP TIME 10 minutes   **COOK TIME** 15 minutes

In a small bowl, mix ½ finely chopped **onion**, 500g **5% fat beef mince** and 1 lightly beaten **egg** until combined. Add 25g crumbled **Stilton** and mix gently to combine. Shape the mixture into 4 patties about 2cm thick. Mist a griddle pan or frying pan with **calorie controlled cooking spray** and put over a medium heat. Cook the burgers for 15 minutes, turning occasionally, until cooked through. Crumble another 25g Stilton over the burgers for the final 2 minutes of cooking time. Serve each burger on a toasted **rye sandwich thin** with **spinach** leaves, sliced **apple** and sliced **red onion**.

SmartPoints
8 per burger

ROSEMARY & THYME SANDWICH BURGER

Makes 4

PREP TIME 15 minutes   **COOK TIME** 10 minutes

In a small bowl, mix ½ finely chopped **onion**, 500g **5% fat pork mince**, 1 tablespoon finely chopped **fresh rosemary**, 1 tablespoon chopped **fresh thyme**, ½ teaspoon lightly crushed **fennel seeds** and 1 lightly beaten **egg** until well combined. Shape the mixture into 4 patties about 1.5cm thick. Mist a griddle pan or frying pan with **calorie controlled cooking spray** and put over a medium heat. Cook the burgers for 10 minutes, turning occasionally, until cooked through. Sandwich each burger between two slices of toasted **Weight Watchers Thick Sliced Wholemeal Bread** with ½ teaspoon English **mustard** and **lettuce** leaves.

SmartPoints
8 per burger

THAI-STYLE BURGER

Makes 4

PREP TIME 15 minutes   **COOK TIME** 15 minutes

In a small bowl, mix ½ finely chopped **onion**, 500g **5% fat pork mince**, 1 finely chopped **lemon grass** stalk, 1 deseeded and finely chopped **red chilli**, 1 tablespoon peeled and grated **fresh ginger**, 2 tablespoons chopped **fresh mint**, the grated zest of 1 **lime**, 2 teaspoons **fish sauce** and 1 lightly beaten **egg** until combined. Shape the mixture into 4 patties about 2cm thick. Mist a griddle pan or frying pan with **calorie controlled cooking spray** and put over a medium heat. Cook the burgers for 15 minutes, turning occasionally, or until cooked through. Mix 1 tablespoon reduced-fat **mayonnaise** with 1 teaspoon **sweet chilli sauce**. Serve each burger in a small, **seeded wholemeal roll** with extra **mint leaves**, shredded **cabbage**, grated **carrot** and the chilli mayo.

SmartPoints
8 per burger

HARISSA BURGER
Makes 4
PREP TIME 10 minutes   **COOK TIME** 15 minutes

In a small bowl, mix ½ finely chopped **onion**, 500g **5% fat beef mince**, 1 tablespoon **harissa paste**, the grated zest of 1 **lemon** and 1 lightly beaten **egg** until combined. Shape the mixture into 4 patties about 2cm thick. Mist a griddle pan or frying pan with **calorie controlled cooking spray** and put over a medium heat. Cook the burgers for 15 minutes, turning occasionally, until cooked through. Serve each burger in a small folded **flatbread**, with **cucumber** ribbons and 1 tablespoon **0% fat natural Greek yogurt**.

9 SmartPoints
value · 9 per burger

STIR-FRIED BEEF WITH MANGO

A colourful stir-fry that's packed with fresh flavours and spiced up with chilli.

Serves 4
PREP TIME 20 minutes
COOK TIME 20 minutes

Ingredients
200g brown basmati rice
400g thin-cut sirloin steak, fat
  trimmed, cut into strips
1½ tablespoons soy sauce
2 garlic cloves, finely chopped
4cm-piece fresh ginger, grated
2 teaspoons toasted sesame oil
200g sugar snap peas
1 red chilli, deseeded and
  finely chopped
3 spring onions, finely sliced
1 mango, peeled, stone removed
  and cut into thin wedges
Handful fresh coriander,
  roughly chopped

 SmartPoints
8 per serving

 See page 6

Method

1 Cook the rice to pack instructions. Meanwhile, put the steak in a bowl with the soy sauce, garlic and ginger, then toss to coat.

2 Heat the oil in a large non-stick wok or frying pan over a high heat. Add half the steak and stir-fry for 1 minute or until the beef is browned. Transfer the cooked steak to a plate, then stir-fry the rest of the meat. Remove from the pan and set aside.

3 Add the sugar snap peas and 2 tablespoons water to the pan and stir-fry for 1 minute until just tender. Add the chilli and spring onions and cook for 1 minute, then return the steak to the pan with the mango and toss to combine and warm through.

4 Scatter over the coriander and serve with the cooked rice.

 ### COCONUT RICE
Instead of the boiled basmati rice, try this with coconut rice (p138), for a total of **13 SmartPoints** per serving.

 ### CRISPY ONIONS
Scatter 25g crispy onions over the stir-fry before serving for an extra **1 SmartPoint** per serving.

Meat

PORK, APPLE & WHITE BEAN STEW

This easy one-pot dish is great when you're having guests for dinner.

Serves 6
PREP TIME 20 minutes
COOK TIME 50 minutes

Ingredients
2 teaspoons olive oil
500g pork tenderloin, trimmed
  of fat and cut into chunks
1 tablespoon plain flour
5 shallots, halved
2 garlic cloves, finely chopped
3 Granny Smith apples, peeled,
  cored and cut into chunks
500ml chicken stock, made with
  1 stock cube
400g tin haricot beans, drained
  and rinsed
2 sprigs of fresh rosemary
1 tablespoon sage, roughly chopped
200g sourdough bread, torn
  into chunks

 SmartPoints
5 per serving

Method
1 Put 1 teaspoon of the oil in a flameproof lidded casserole and set over a medium heat. Toss the pork in the flour and fry for 4-5 minutes until browned, but not cooked through. Remove from the casserole and set aside.

2 Add the shallots to the casserole and cook for 5 minutes until beginning to brown – add a splash of water if it starts to stick. Add the garlic and apples and cook for 1 minute. Add a little of the stock and stir with a wooden spoon to deglaze the casserole. Stir in the remaining stock, then return the pork to the casserole, with the beans, rosemary and sage. Bring to a boil, then reduce the heat and simmer, uncovered, for 15 minutes.

3 Preheat the oven to 190°C, fan 170°C, gas mark 5. Toss the bread with the remaining oil and season to taste. Top the stew with the bread and bake for 15-20 minutes until the bread is golden brown and the stew is bubbling.

 ### CREME FRAICHE
Add
For a creamier dish, stir 2 tablespoons 0% fat crème fraîche into the stew before topping it with the bread for no additional **SmartPoints**.

 ### CELERIAC, POTATO & PARSNIP MASH
Side
Try serving this with celeriac, potato & parsnip mash (p137) for an extra **4 SmartPoints** per serving.

COTTAGE PIE POTATOES

A clever twist on a cottage pie – the meat is served in the potatoes.

Makes 4
PREP TIME 5 minutes
COOK TIME 55 minutes

Ingredients
4 x 200g baking potatoes
Calorie controlled cooking spray
1 small onion, finely diced
1 stick celery, finely diced
250g 5% fat beef mince
250ml beef stock, made
  with ½ stock cube
1 tablespoon tomato purée
Few drops Worcestershire sauce
½ teaspoon dried thyme
75ml semi-skimmed milk

 SmartPoints
7 per potato

 See page 6

Method

1 Pierce the skin of the potatoes with a fork in several places, then put them on a microwave-safe plate. Microwave on high for 4 minutes, then turn the potatoes over and microwave for a further 4 minutes until tender. Set aside to cool.

2 Meanwhile, mist a large pan with cooking spray and put over a medium heat. Add the onion and celery and cook for 5 minutes until soft. Turn up the heat to medium-high, add the mince and cook for 5 minutes until brown.

3 Stir in the stock, tomato purée, Worcestershire sauce and thyme. Season to taste, then reduce the heat and simmer for 15-20 minutes until the sauce has thickened.

4 Preheat the oven to 200°C, fan 180°C, gas mark 6. Slice the tops off the potatoes. Scoop the flesh out into a bowl, leaving the skin and a 1cm border of potato. Mash the scooped out potato with the milk and season to taste.

5 Fill the potato skins with the mince mixture, then top with the mash. Transfer to a baking tray and bake for 20-25 minutes until golden, then serve.

 ## HARISSA
Add 2 teaspoons harissa with the stock for no additional **SmartPoints** per serving.

 ## CHEDDAR CHEESE
Top each potato with 10g grated half-fat Cheddar before baking for no additional **SmartPoints** per serving

Meat

ROAST PORK WITH NOODLE SALAD

Sticky, sweet roast pork served with a punchy rice noodle salad.

Serves 4

PREP TIME 20 minutes,
plus marinating
COOK TIME 25 minutes

Ingredients

2 tablespoons soy sauce
1 tablespoon tomato purée
1 tablespoon clear honey
2cm-piece fresh ginger, grated
1 teaspoon Chinese five spice
  powder
500g pork tenderloin, fat trimmed
100g flat rice noodles
2 tablespoons rice wine vinegar
Juice of 1 lime
2 teaspoons toasted sesame oil
1 teaspoon toasted sesame seeds
Small handful fresh coriander,
  chopped
1 carrot, peeled into ribbons
1 cucumber, peeled into ribbons

 SmartPoints
7 per serving

GF See page 6

Method

1 Put the soy sauce, tomato purée, honey, ginger and five spice powder in a shallow bowl and stir to combine. Add the pork and turn to coat in the marinade, then cover with clingfilm and chill in the fridge for 1 hour.

2 Preheat the oven to 200°C, fan 180°C, gas mark 6. Set a large ovenproof frying pan over a medium heat. Lift the pork from the marinade and sear on all sides, basting with the marinade as you go. Transfer to the oven and roast for 20 minutes until cooked through, basting with the juices every 5 minutes.

3 Meanwhile, soak the noodles in hot water until soft. Drain and rinse in cold water, then set aside.

4 In a small bowl, whisk together the vinegar, lime juice and sesame oil, then stir in the sesame seeds and coriander. Put the noodles, carrot and cucumber in a large bowl, drizzle over the dressing and toss to combine.

5 Slice the pork and serve with the noodle salad.

 ## SATAY SAUCE
Try serving this with satay sauce (p138) for an extra **3 SmartPoints** per serving.

Garlic croutons
+ 3 SmartPoints
per serving

Celeriac, potato & parsnip mash
+ 4 SmartPoints
per serving

Carrot & harissa houmous
+ 4 SmartPoints
per serving

Meat
SIDES

Tired of the same-old accompaniments?
Try these side dishes with a difference,
perfect for serving with meat.

Tomato & red onion salad
+ 3 SmartPoints
per serving

GARLIC CROUTONS
Serves 4

PREP TIME 5 minutes
COOK TIME 20 minutes

Preheat the oven to 200°C,
fan 180°C, gas mark 6. Put 150g
cubed **sourdough bread** in a bowl
and mist with **calorie controlled
cooking spray**. Scatter over
1 teaspoon **garlic granules** and
½ teaspoon dried **oregano**, season
to taste and toss together. Spread
out on a baking sheet and bake
for 18-20 minutes, tossing halfway
through, until crisp and golden.

 SmartPoints
3 per serving ⓥ

CELERIAC, POTATO & PARSNIP MASH
Serves 8

PREP TIME 20 minutes
COOK TIME 35 minutes

Put 1 peeled and cubed **celeriac**,
3 peeled and roughly chopped
parsnips and 2 roughly chopped
potatoes in a pan and cover with
water. Bring to a boil, reduce
the heat, cover, and simmer for
15 minutes. Remove the potatoes
and cook the remaining veg for
a further 15-20 minutes or until
tender. Drain. Mash the potato with
a potato masher. Cover and keep
warm. Transfer the parsnip and
celeriac to a food processor and
blend until smooth. Add the purée
to the potato and combine. Stir in
100g half-fat **crème fraîche** and
1 teaspoon **Dijon mustard**, then
season to taste and serve.

 SmartPoints
4 per serving

ⓥ GF See page 6

TOMATO & RED ONION SALAD
Serves 4
PREP TIME 10 minutes

Layer 500g sliced mixed **tomatoes** with ½ a thinly sliced small **red onion** on a serving plate, then scatter over 25g roughly chopped **walnuts** and 40g **pomegranate** seeds. Whisk together 1 tablespoon **extra virgin olive oil** and the juice of ½ **orange**, season and drizzle over the salad, then serve.

 SmartPoints
3 per serving

  See page 6

CARROT & HARISSA HOUMOUS
Serves 4
PREP TIME 15 minutes
COOK TIME 25 minutes

Put two large chopped **carrots** in a medium pan, pour in 500ml **vegetable stock**, then boil for 25 minutes until tender. In a food processor, blitz 3 **garlic cloves**, the juice of 1 **lemon** and 1 teaspoon **salt** until the garlic is chopped. Add 1 x 400g tin rinsed and drained **chickpeas**, the carrots, 75g **tahini** and ¼ teaspoon **ground cumin** and process, gradually adding 150ml ice cold water until the mixture is smooth and thick. Add 2 tablespoon **harissa** and process until combined.

 SmartPoints
4 per serving

  See page 6

COCONUT RICE
Serves 4
PREP TIME 5 minutes
COOK TIME 10 minutes

Rinse 250g **basmati rice** and put in a pan with 500ml **coconut drink** (we used Alpro). Season to taste, bring to a boil, then reduce the heat, cover and simmer for 6 minutes. Turn off the heat and leave for 10 minutes. Meanwhile, heat a pan over a medium heat. Add 2 tablespoons **desiccated coconut** and stir until golden brown. Once the rice is cooked, stir through the coconut and serve.

 SmartPoints
9 per serving

  See page 6

SATAY SAUCE
Serves 4
PREP TIME 5 minutes

In a small jug, whisk together 50g crunchy **peanut butter**, the juice of 1 **lime**, 1 tablespoon **soy sauce**, 1 tablespoon **sweet chilli sauce**, 1 tablespoon freshly grated **ginger** and 1 finely chopped **garlic clove** and 2-3 tablespoons hot water until you have a smooth sauce.

 SmartPoints
3 per serving

  See page 6

Satay sauce
+ 3 SmartPoints
per serving

Coconut rice
+ 9 SmartPoints
per serving

Veggie

Veggie

HALLOUMI BURGER WITH CARAMELISED ONIONS

This breadless burger uses portobello mushrooms instead of buns.

Makes 4
PREP TIME 10 minutes
COOK TIME 30 minutes

Ingredients
8 large portobello mushrooms,
  stalks removed
1 tablespoon olive oil
½ tablespoon low-fat spread
3 red onions, finely sliced
1 tablespoon balsamic vinegar
½ tablespoon light brown sugar
Calorie controlled cooking spray
250g light halloumi, cut
  into 4 rounds
80g rocket leaves

 SmartPoints
8 per burger

  See page 6

Method
1 Preheat the oven to 200°C, fan 180°C, gas mark 6.
Put the mushrooms, stem side down, on a large baking
tray and brush with the oil. Season to taste and roast
for 25-30 minutes, turning over halfway through.

2 Meanwhile, heat the low-fat spread in a large pan over
a medium heat and fry the onions for 6-8 minutes, or until
soft. Add the balsamic vinegar and sugar and continue to
cook for a further 10 minutes, or until sticky. Season well
and set aside.

3 Mist a large frying pan with cooking spray and cook
the halloumi slices for 2-3 minutes on each side, or
until golden brown.

4 Serve the halloumi slices between 2 mushroom
'buns', topped with the caramelised onions and
the rocket leaves.

Side ## SPICY CHILLI CHIPS
Serve the burger with spicy chilli chips (p79),
for an extra **2 SmartPoints** per serving.

Side ## COURGETTE SALAD
Serve this with the courgette salad (p165),
for an extra **4 SmartPoints** per serving.

GREEK-STYLE ORZO SALAD

Try this easy pasta salad for a quick and tasty lunch.

Serves 4
PREP TIME 5 minutes
COOK TIME 12 minutes

Ingredients
280g orzo pasta
200g cherry tomatoes, halved
1 small cucumber, diced
50g pitted black olives
1 tablespoon extra virgin olive oil
Grated zest and juice of 1 lemon
75g light feta, crumbled

 SmartPoints
10 per serving

Method

1 Cook the pasta in a pan of boiling water for 10-12 minutes until al dente. Drain and run under cold water to cool. Drain again, transfer to a bowl and add the tomatoes, cucumber, olives.

2 Whisk together the olive oil, lemon zest and juice, then season well. Pour the dressing over the salad and stir well to combine. Scatter over the feta and serve.

 ## SUNDRIED TOMATOES

Add 50g chopped sundried tomatoes (not in oil), to the salad for an extra **1 SmartPoint** per serving.

 ## GARLIC CROUTONS

Try serving the salad with garlic croutons (p137) for an extra **3 SmartPoints** per serving.

INDIAN-SPICED PANEER PANCAKES

Chickpea flour pancakes with a spicy spinach and cheese filling.

Makes 4
PREP TIME 15 minutes
COOK TIME 25 minutes

For the pancakes
150g chickpea flour
1cm-piece fresh ginger, grated
1 teaspoon ground turmeric
1 green chilli, deseeded and
  finely chopped
Handful fresh coriander,
  finely chopped
2 teaspoons rapeseed oil

For the filling
½ tablespoon rapeseed oil
1 onion, finely sliced
1 garlic clove, finely sliced
175g paneer, cut into small chunks
2 teaspoons garam masala
200g young leaf spinach
2 tablespoons 0% fat natural yogurt
Small handful fresh coriander,
  roughly chopped

 SmartPoints
10 per pancake

  See page 6

Method

1 To make the pancakes, put the flour in a bowl and slowly whisk in 200ml water until you have a smooth batter, then add the ginger, turmeric, chilli and coriander.

2 Heat 1 teaspoon of the rapeseed oil in a small non-stick frying pan over a medium-high heat. Ladle in ¼ of the batter and cook for 2 minutes, or until golden underneath. Flip and continue to cook for a further minute. Remove from the pan and repeat until you have used all of the batter – use the remaining teaspoon of rapeseed oil if needed. Stack the pancakes between pieces of baking paper and keep warm in a low oven until ready to serve.

3 To make the filling, heat the ½ tablespoon rapeseed oil in a large frying pan and fry the onions for 6-8 minutes until soft. Add the garlic and cook for 1 minute. Toss the paneer in the garam masala, then add to the pan and cook for 4-5 minutes. Add the spinach and let it wilt, then stir through the yogurt.

4 Put a quarter of the filling in the middle of each pancake, scatter over the coriander, then fold to serve.

 Side

TZATZIKI
Serve this with tzatziki (p34) for no additional **SmartPoints** per serving.

 Side

LEMON & ALMOND RICE
This is great served with lemon & almond rice (p165), for an extra **6 SmartPoints** per serving.

4 QUICK CHICKPEA IDEAS

Tinned chickpeas are a great veggie storecupboard standby that can be used in lots of ways. Try them in these easy recipes…

SPICED ROAST CHICKPEAS

Serves 4

PREP TIME 5 minutes **COOK TIME** 30 minutes

Preheat the oven to 200°C, fan 180°C, gas mark 6. Drain and rinse a 400g tin **chickpeas** and dry them on kitchen paper. Put in a roasting tin and toss with 1 teaspoon smoked **paprika**, 1 teaspoon ground **cumin** and 1 teaspoon ground **coriander**. Drizzle over 1 tablespoon **olive oil** and stir well so the chickpeas are coated. Roast for 30 minutes or until crisp, then serve as a snack.

 SmartPoints
1 per serving See page 6

CHICKPEA & GOAT'S CHEESE SALAD

Serves 4

PREP TIME 5 minutes

Drain and rinse 2 x 400g tins of **chickpeas** and place in a large serving bowl with 400g halved cherry **tomatoes** and 70g **rocket**. Whisk together 1 tablespoon **extra virgin olive oil**, the grated zest and juice of 1 **lemon** and 1 teaspoon dried **oregano**. Pour over the salad and toss to combine, then season to taste. Toss through 150g roughly chopped **goat's cheese**, then serve.

 SmartPoints
6 per serving See page 6

CORIANDER & LIME HOUMOUS

Serves 4

PREP TIME 5 minutes

Drain and rinse a 400g tin **chickpeas**, then put in a food processor with 1 large **garlic clove**, 2 tablespoons **0% fat natural Greek yogurt**, 1 tablespoon **tahini**, ½ tablespoon **olive oil**, the juice of 1 **lime**, a handful of **fresh coriander** and 2 tablespoons water. Blitz until you have a chunky textured houmous. Add more water if you prefer it smoother. Serve with vegetable crudités for a simple snack.

 **SmartPoints**
1 per serving See page 6

CHICKPEA & TOMATO SOUP

Serves 4

PREP TIME 10 minutes **COOK TIME** 10 minutes

Drain and rinse 1 x 400g tin **chickpeas** and put in a pan with 1 x 400g tin chopped **tomatoes**, 100g **cherry tomatoes**, 300ml hot **vegetable stock** made with 1 stock cube, 1 chopped **garlic clove**, 1 teaspoon ground **coriander**, ½ teaspoon ground **cinnamon** and ½ teaspoon **chilli powder**. Squeeze in the juice of 1 **lime**, then blitz with a stick blender until smooth. Gently heat through, season to taste and serve, or chill in the fridge and serve cold with 1 teaspoon **0% fat natural yogurt** swirled through each serving.

 **SmartPoints**
0 per serving See page 6

Veggie

QUORN, CAULIFLOWER & SPINACH CURRY

An easy curry that's great served with rice or naan bread.

Serves 4
PREP TIME 15 minutes
COOK TIME 40 minutes

Ingredients
1 teaspoon cumin seeds
1 teaspoon mustard seeds
1 teaspoon ground coriander
½ teaspoon ground ginger
½ teaspoon ground turmeric
1 tablespoon vegetable oil
1 onion, finely sliced
2 garlic cloves, finely sliced
1 green chilli, deseeded and
  finely chopped
1cm-piece fresh ginger, grated
4 tomatoes, roughly chopped
½ head cauliflower, broken
  into small florets
350g Quorn pieces
250ml vegetable stock, made
  with 1 stock cube
120g young leaf spinach
Handful of fresh coriander,
  roughly chopped

 SmartPoints
2 per serving

 See page 6

Method
1 Toast the cumin and mustard seeds in a dry frying pan over a medium heat until they start to pop. Crush using a pestle and mortar and mix with the other spices.

2 Heat the oil in a large frying pan and cook the onion for 6-8 minutes, or until soft. Add the garlic, chilli and ginger and cook for a further 2 minutes, then add the spice mixture, along with the tomatoes. Cook for 4-5 minutes, then add the cauliflower and Quorn. Stir to coat, then add the stock. Bring to the boil, then reduce to a simmer. Simmer for 15 minutes, partially covered, or until the cauliflower is tender, but not too soft.

3 Stir through the spinach and cook until it wilts. Season to taste, then stir through the coriander and serve.

 COCONUT MILK
Replace 150ml of the stock with 150ml reduced-fat coconut milk, for an extra **1 SmartPoint** per serving.

 LEMON & ALMOND RICE
Try serving this with lemon & almond rice (p165) for an extra **6 SmartPoints** per serving.

 NAAN BREAD
This is also great served with warmed mini naan breads, instead of rice, for an extra **3 SmartPoints** per serving.

TURMERIC & YOGURT MARINATED TOFU

This spicy tofu is served with a simple lentil salad and topped with almonds.

Serves 4

PREP TIME 10 minutes,
plus marinating
COOK TIME 45-50 minutes

For the tofu

400g tofu
150g 0% fat natural yogurt
1 teaspoon ground cumin
1 teaspoon ground coriander
1 teaspoon ground turmeric
1 teaspoon chilli flakes
Juice of ½ lemon
2 garlic cloves, crushed
1 tablespoon vegetable oil

For the lentil salad

4 red onions, cut into
   thin wedges
½ tablespoon rapeseed oil
2 x 400g tins green lentils,
   drained and rinsed
30g sultanas
Handful of fresh coriander,
   roughly chopped
25g toasted flaked almonds

 SmartPoints
5 per serving

  See page 6

Method

1 Drain the tofu, then wrap it in kitchen paper and put it on a plate with a second plate plate on top. Weigh it down with one of the tins of lentils and leave for 30 minutes to allow any extra moisture to drain out, then cut into 8 thick slices.

2 Meanwhile, in a bowl, whisk together the remaining tofu ingredients except the oil. Add the tofu slices and toss together. Cover and set aside in the fridge to marinate for at least 30 minutes.

3 Preheat the oven to 200°C, fan 180°C, gas mark 6. Put the onions in a roasting tin, drizzle with the oil and roast for 25-30 minutes, or until soft. Remove from the oven and transfer to a bowl, then add the lentils, sultanas and fresh coriander, and toss to combine.

4 To cook the tofu, heat 1 tablespoon oil in a large non-stick frying pan. Fry the tofu for 3-4 minutes on each side, until golden. Serve with the lentil salad and the almonds scattered over.

 ### TZATZIKI
Serve this with tzatziki (p34) for no additional **SmartPoints** per serving.

 ### PANEER
Add 60g diced paneer to the salad, for an extra **2 SmartPoints** per serving.

SPRING VEGETABLE RISOTTO

Plenty of green veg gives this easy risotto loads of fresh flavour.

Serves 4
PREP TIME 5 minutes
COOK TIME 20-25 minutes

Ingredients
2 teaspoons olive oil
2 onions, finely chopped
2 garlic cloves, finely sliced
250g risotto rice
1 litre hot vegetable stock,
   made with 2 stock cubes
150g frozen peas
200g broad beans
150g asparagus, trimmed
Handful of fresh mint leaves,
   finely shredded

 SmartPoints
8 per serving

 See page 6

Method

1 Heat the oil in a large frying pan and cook the onions for 6-8 minutes, or until soft. Add the garlic and cook over a medium heat for 1 minute. Add the rice and stir to coat.

2 Add a ladleful of stock and cook, stirring, until most of the liquid has been absorbed. Repeat until you have used two-thirds of the stock – this should take about 15 minutes.

3 Add the vegetables to the risotto and continue to cook as before until all of the stock has been used, the rice is al dente and the vegetables are cooked. Season to taste, then stir in the mint and serve.

 ### GOAT'S CHEESE
Stir through 35g goat's cheese at the end until melted, for an extra **1 SmartPoint** per serving.

 ### PESTO
Serve this with pesto (p166), for an extra **4 SmartPoints** per serving.

Veggie

5 PASTA SAUCES

Pasta is the perfect base for veggie meals. Try these tasty ideas.

PEA PESTO

Serves 4

PREP TIME 5 minutes   **COOK TIME** 15 minutes

Cook 125g fresh or frozen **peas** for 3-4 minutes in a pan of boiling water. Drain and rinse in cold water to cool. Put in a mini food processor with 2 **garlic cloves**, 15g grated **vegetarian Italian hard cheese**, a handful of **fresh basil**, the juice of 1 **lemon** and 1 tablespoon **extra virgin olive oil** and blitz to a purée. Add a splash of water if the pesto is too thick. Cook 240g **wholewheat pasta** to pack instructions, then toss with the pesto to serve.

7 SmartPoints
SmartPoints value · 7 per serving **V**

ROASTED TOMATO & BASIL

Serves 4

PREP TIME 5 minutes   **COOK TIME** 1 hour 15 minutes

Preheat the oven to 180°C, fan 160°C, gas mark 4. Put 1kg halved mixed **tomatoes** in a large roasting tin with 2 **garlic cloves** and season to taste. Combine 1 tablespoon **olive oil**, 1 tablespoon **balsamic vinegar**, a pinch of **chilli flakes** and a pinch of **caster sugar** in a small jug, then drizzle over the tomatoes. Roast for 50 minutes-1 hour, or until the tomatoes are soft and starting to caramelise. Remove from the oven, roughly crush with a fork and stir through a handful of torn **fresh basil** leaves. Cook 240g **wholewheat pasta** to pack instructions, stir through the sauce and serve.

7 SmartPoints
SmartPoints value
7 per serving ✳ Ⓥ

CHICKPEA BOLOGNESE
Serves 4

PREP TIME 10 minutes   **COOK TIME** 40 minutes

Preheat the oven to 200°C, fan 180°C, gas mark 6. Drain and rinse 2 x 400g tins **chickpeas**. Put in a roasting tin, season and toss with 1 teaspoon dried **mixed herbs** and 1 tablespoon **olive oil**. Roast for 30 minutes. Meanwhile, heat 1 tablespoon olive oil in a large pan and fry 1 finely sliced **onion**, 1 chopped **carrot** and 1 chopped **celery** stick for 8-10 minutes, or until soft. Add 2 sliced **garlic cloves**, 1 tablespoon chopped **fresh rosemary** and 1 tablespoon **tomato purée**. Cook for 2 minutes. Add 2 x 400g tins chopped **tomatoes** and 1 tablespoon **balsamic vinegar**. Simmer for 20-25 minutes, or until reduced. Toss the chickpeas through the sauce. Cook 240g **wholewheat pasta** to pack instructions and serve with the Bolognese, topped with 2 tablespoons grated **vegetarian Italian hard cheese**.

SmartPoints
9 per serving

BUTTERNUT SQUASH & CHILLI
Serves 4

PREP TIME 15 minutes   **COOK TIME** 55 minutes

Preheat the oven to 200°C, fan 180°C, gas mark 6. Peel and deseed 1 large **butternut squash** then cut it into cubes. Put it in a roasting tin with 3 **garlic cloves** and drizzle with 1 tablespoon **olive oil**. Roast in the oven for 35-40 minutes, or until soft. Remove from the oven and put two-thirds of the squash in a food processor with 300ml **vegetable stock** made from 1 stock cube, 2 tablespoons **0% fat crème fraiche** and 1 deseeded and finely chopped **red chilli**. Blitz to a smooth sauce, adding more stock if you need to. Season to taste. Cook 240g **wholewheat pasta** to pack instructions and serve with the sauce and the remaining roasted squash.

SmartPoints
10 per serving

CREAMY MUSHROOM
Serves 4
PREP TIME 10 minutes   **COOK TIME** 20 minutes

Heat 1 tablespoon **olive oil** in a large frying pan and fry 2 finely chopped **shallots** for 3-4 minutes, or until soft. Add 2 finely sliced **garlic cloves** and cook for 2 minutes, then add 600g sliced mixed **mushrooms** and a small handful of **fresh thyme** leaves and cook for 10 minutes, or until the mushrooms are golden. Add 90g **light cream cheese** and stir until melted, then season to taste. Cook 240g **wholewheat pasta** to pack instructions and serve with the mushroom sauce and garnished with extra thyme.

7 SmartPoints
SmartPoints value   **SmartPoints**
7 per serving (V)

Veggie

MEDITERRANEAN VEGETABLE PASTA BAKE

A tasty all-in-one meal that's packed with fresh vegetables.

Serves 4
PREP TIME 15 minutes
COOK TIME 45 minutes

Ingredients
2 red onions, cut into wedges
3 mixed peppers, deseeded and
   cut into large chunks
2 courgettes, cut into thick rounds
1 small aubergine, cut into chunks
2 tablespoons olive oil
2 garlic cloves
2 x 400g tins chopped tomatoes
1 tablespoon balsamic vinegar
1 teaspoon clear honey
240g wholewheat penne pasta
Handful fresh basil leaves
50g vegetarian hard Italian
   cheese, grated

 SmartPoints
10 per serving

Method

1 Preheat the oven to 200°C, fan 180°C, gas mark 6.
   Put the onions, peppers, courgettes and aubergine
   in a large roasting tin, drizzle with 1 tablespoon of
   the oil and toss to coat. Roast for 25-30 minutes,
   or until tender.

2 Meanwhile, heat the remaining oil in a large saucepan
   over a low heat and fry the garlic for 1 minute, then add
   the tomatoes, balsamic vinegar and honey and bring to
   the boil. Partially cover and simmer for 15-20 minutes,
   or until the sauce has reduced. Remove from the heat
   and season to taste.

3 Cook the pasta in a pan of boiling water for 10 minutes
   until al dente. Drain, then combine with the tomato sauce
   and roasted vegetables. Stir through the basil, then transfer
   to a baking dish and scatter over the cheese. Bake for
   15 minutes, or until the cheese is melted and golden.

QUORN SAUSAGES
Add
Add 4 Quorn vegetarian sausages to the
roasting tin with the vegetables. When
cooked, cut into bite-size chunks, then
add to the pasta mixture before baking,
for an extra **1 SmartPoint** per serving.

GARLIC & HERB BREADCRUMBS
Side
Sprinkle over garlic & herb breadcrumbs (p166)
for an extra **2 SmartPoints** per serving.

Veggie

ROASTED SQUASH & FREEKEH SALAD

A Middle Eastern-style salad with the nutty, earth flavours of freekeh.

Serves 4

PREP TIME 15 minutes
COOK TIME 35 minutes

Ingredients

1 large butternut squash, peeled
  deseeded and cubed
1 tablespoon olive oil
1 teaspoon ras el hanout
250g freekeh
Handful each of fresh dill, parsley
  and mint, roughly chopped
1 tablespoon extra virgin olive oil
1 tablespoon pomegranate molasses
Juice of 1 lemon
100g pomegranate seeds
75g light feta, crumbled

 SmartPoints
10 per serving

Method

1 Preheat the oven to 200°C, fan 180°C, gas mark 6.
  Put the squash in a roasting tin and drizzle over the olive
  oil. Scatter over the ras el hanout and season to taste.
  Toss together, then roast for 30-35 minutes, or until
  tender. Remove from the oven and set aside to cool.

2 Meanwhile, put the freekeh in a large pan with 600ml
  water. Bring to the boil and cook for 15-20 minutes,
  until tender. Drain and rinse in cold water.

3 In a large bowl, mix together the herbs and cooked
  freekeh. Whisk together the oil, pomegranate molasses
  and lemon juice, then pour over the salad. Add the
  squash, pomegranate seeds and feta, season to taste
  and toss to combine all the ingredients, then serve.

 TOASTED
PUMPKIN SEEDS
Sprinkle over 1 tablespoon toasted pumpkin
seeds per person when serving, for an extra
2 SmartPoints per serving.

 TOASTED
HERBY PITTAS
Try serving this with toasted herby pittas (p166)
for an extra **4 SmartPoints** per serving.

Toasted herby pittas
+ 4 SmartPoints per serving

Garlic & herb breadcrumbs
+ 2 SmartPoints per serving

Veggie

SIDES

Make vegetarian meals extra special with this selection of simple side dishes and garnishes.

Courgette salad
+ 4 SmartPoints per serving

Lemon & almond rice
+ 6 SmartPoints per serving

COURGETTE SALAD
Serves 4
PREP TIME 10 minutes
COOK TIME 30 minutes

Mist a griddle pan with **calorie controlled cooking spray** and put over a medium heat. Griddle 6 thinly sliced **courgettes** in batches for 2 minutes on each side until tender. Leave to cool. Whisk together 1 tablespoon **extra virgin olive oil** and the juice of 1 **lemon**, then pour over the courgettes. Toss through 35g **sultanas**, 25 toasted **pine nuts** and a handful of torn fresh **basil**. Season to taste, then serve.

 SmartPoints
4 per serving

 See page 6

LEMON & ALMOND RICE
Serves 4
PREP TIME 5 minutes
COOK TIME 30 minutes

Mist a large lidded pan with **calorie controlled cooking spray**, put over a medium heat and fry 1 finely sliced **onion** for 5-6 minutes until soft. Add 2 finely sliced **garlic cloves** and continue to cook for a further 2 minutes. Add 200g **long grain rice** and stir well until the rice is coated. Add 500ml water, along with 4-5 pieces of **lemon peel**. Bring to the boil, then reduce to a simmer, cover and cook for 20 minutes, or until the rice is tender and the water has evaporated. Discard the lemon peel. Season and serve topped with 20g toasted **flaked almonds**.

 SmartPoints
6 per serving

 See page 6

GARLIC & HERB BREADCRUMBS

Serves 4

PREP TIME 5 minutes
COOK TIME 10 minutes

Preheat the oven to 200°C, fan 180°C, gas mark 6. Toss 75g **fresh white breadcrumbs** with 1 crushed **garlic clove**, 1 teaspoon **dried rosemary** and 2 tablespoons grated **vegetarian hard Italian cheese**. Spread them on a baking sheet and mist with **calorie controlled cooking spray**. Toast in the oven for 8-10 minutes, or until golden. Serve scattered over pasta dishes.

  SmartPoints
2 per serving

SOURDOUGH TOASTS

Serves 4

PREP TIME 5 minutes
COOK TIME 10 minutes

Preheat the oven to 200°C, fan 180°C, gas mark 6. Put 120g **sourdough bread**, cut into 8 thin slices, on a baking sheet and mist with **calorie controlled cooking spray**. Season with rock salt, then bake in the oven for 8-10 minutes, or until crisp and golden, turning halfway through. When cooked, remove from the oven and rub the slices with the cut sides of 1 peeled and halved **garlic clove**.

 SmartPoints
2 per serving

TOASTED HERBY PITTAS

Serves 4

PREP TIME 2 minutes
COOK TIME 8 minutes

Preheat the oven to 200°C fan 180°C, gas mark 6. Put 4 **pitta breads** on a large baking tray. Mist with **caloried controlled cooking spray**, then scatter over 1 teaspoon **dried mixed herbs**. Toast in the oven for 5-8 minutes until golden.

  SmartPoints
4 per serving

PESTO

Serves 4

PREP TIME 5 minutes

Put 20g fresh **basil** leaves, 1 tablespoon toasted **pine nuts**, 2 tablespoons grated **vegetarian Italian hard cheese**, the juice of 1 **lemon** and 1 tablespoon **extra virgin olive oil** in a mini food processor and blitz until smooth. Add a splash of water to loosen if the pesto is too thick. Season to taste, then serve.

  SmartPoints
4 per serving

 See page 6

Pesto
+ 4 SmartPoints
per serving

Sourdough toasts
+ 2 SmartPoints
per serving

Snacks,
puds &
drinks

PEACH & PARMA HAM TARTINES

For a simple but tasty snack, try this super speedy open sandwich.

Makes 2
PREP TIME 10 minutes

Ingredients

75g quark
1 garlic clove, crushed
1 tablespoon chopped fresh basil,
  plus extra leaves to serve
1 large ripe peach
1½ teaspoons balsamic vinegar
2 sandwich thins

 **SmartPoints**
6 per tartine

Method

1 In a bowl, mash together the quark, garlic and chopped basil, and season to taste.

2 Halve the peach and remove the stone, then cut each half into 5 wedges. Put into a bowl, drizzle over the balsamic vinegar and toss together to coat.

3 Toast the sandwich thins, then put the two halves together and top with the quark and herb mixture. Add 5 peach wedges, 2 slices of ham and some basil leaves to each thin, then serve.

VEGGIE SCOTCH EGGS

This version of the British classic uses chickpea mash instead of sausagemeat.

Makes 4
PREP TIME 25 minutes, plus chilling
COOK TIME 20 minutes

Ingredients
5 large eggs
4 slices Weight Watchers Wholemeal Bread
400g tin chickpeas, drained and rinsed
1 garlic clove, crushed
½ teaspoon ground mace
Grated zest of ½ lemon
2 teaspoons dried sage
1 tablespoon sunflower oil
2 tablespoons plain flour

4 SmartPoints
4 per scotch egg **V**

Method

1 Put 4 of the eggs in a pan of cold water. Bring to the boil, cook for 5 minutes then transfer immediately to a large bowl of ice-cold water. Once the eggs are cool enough to handle, peel them and set aside.

2 Put one of the slices of bread into a food processor and pulse to crumbs. Pat the drained chickpeas dry with kitchen paper, then add them to the food processor with the breadcrumbs and pulse again until they're finely chopped, but not too smooth. Transfer the mixture to a bowl and stir in the garlic, mace, lemon zest and sage, along with the yolk from the remaining egg, then season to taste and set aside.

3 Toast the 3 remaining slices of bread until golden, then whizz them to crumbs in the food processor and tip onto a large plate. Drizzle over the oil and rub in with your fingertips to coat all the breadcrumbs in the oil.

4 Put the flour onto a second plate and roll one of the peeled eggs in it, shaking off any excess. Take a quarter of the chickpea mixture, flatten it between your hands and wrap it around the floured egg, moulding so it completely covers the egg in an even layer with no gaps. Repeat with the remaining boiled eggs.

5 In a small bowl, beat the remaining egg white with a fork and brush over each of the chickpea coated eggs, then roll them in the toasted breadcrumbs. Put the coated eggs on a baking sheet and chill for 1 hour.

6 Preheat the oven to 200°C, fan 180°C, gas mark 6. Bake the eggs for 18-20 minutes until the crumb coating is crisp and golden.

GREEK SALAD SKEWERS

Try this simple idea for an appetiser to serve with drinks before dinner.

Serves 4
PREP TIME 10 minutes,
plus marinating

Ingredients
120g light feta, cut into 12 cubes
¼ teaspoon fennel seeds
¼ teaspoon dried oregano
Grated zest of 1 lemon, plus the
 juice of ½
12 small cherry tomatoes
12cm piece cucumber, cut
 into 12 chunks
12 small, pitted black olives

You will also need
12 small skewers or cocktail sticks

 **SmartPoints**
2 per serving

   See page 6

Method
1 Put the feta in a small, shallow bowl. In a pestle and mortar, crush the fennel and oregano and season with black pepper. If you don't have a pestle and mortar, use the end of a rolling pin and a small bowl.

2 Stir the lemon zest and juice into the spices, then drizzle over the feta cubes. Turn the cubes to coat, then leave to marinate for 30 minutes, turning again twice more.

3 Thread the marinated feta onto each of the skewers, followed by a cherry tomato, a cube of cucumber and an olive. Serve 3 skewers per person.

CRISPY GREEN BEAN 'FRIES'

Inspired by Japanese tempura, these beans have a crispy polenta coating.

Serves 4
PREP TIME 10 minutes
COOK TIME 20 minutes

Ingredients
75g polenta
2 teaspoons garlic granules
200g fine green beans
1 large egg, beaten
Calorie controlled cooking spray

For the dipping sauce
200g passata
2 tablespoons tomato purée
1 red chilli, deseeded and
   finely chopped
1 tablespoon balsamic vinegar

SmartPoints
3 per serving

  See page 6

Method

1 Preheat the oven to 220°C, fan 200°C, gas mark 7.
To make the sauce, put all the sauce ingredients in
a small pan over a medium heat and bring to a boil.
Reduce the heat to low, then cover and simmer for
5 minutes. Remove from the heat and set aside to cool.

2 Mix the polenta with the garlic granules and season to
taste. Pour the egg onto a dinner plate and put the polenta
mixture on another. Put half of the green beans in the
egg to coat, drain any excess, then toss in the polenta – it
doesn't matter if the coating is a bit patchy. Mist a large
baking sheet with cooking spray, then spread out the
beans on it. Repeat with the remaining beans.

3 Mist the tops of the beans with more cooking spray and
bake for 10 minutes, then turn and bake for 2-5 minutes
until the coating is crisp and golden.

4 Serve the beans straight away with the dipping sauce.

MINI SWEETCORN & FETA FRITTERS

Entertaining guests? Serve these mini bites as a starter or canapé.

Serves 6

PREP TIME 10 minutes
COOK TIME 15 minutes

Ingredients

50g plain flour
½ teaspoon baking powder
2 large eggs
198g tin sweetcorn, drained
1 tablespoon sunflower oil
50g light feta
125g 0% fat natural Greek yogurt
3 tablespoons snipped fresh chives

 SmartPoints
2 per serving

Method

1 Put the flour, baking powder, eggs and ¼ of the sweetcorn in a food processor and whizz to a smooth batter. Transfer to a bowl, then stir in the rest of the corn and season to taste.

2 Heat a non-stick frying pan over a medium-low heat. Use kitchen paper and a little of the oil to grease the pan then, in batches, cook tablespoonfuls of the mixture for 2 minutes on each side until golden and cooked through. Repeat, oiling the pan in between each batch until you have 18 fritters. Set aside and keep warm.

3 Put the feta, yogurt and half the chives into a food processor and whizz to a smooth sauce.

4 To serve, put the fritters on a serving plate and top each with some of the yogurt mixture. Scatter over the rest of the chives to garnish. The fritters can be frozen for up to 2 months.

COURGETTE & CHEESE CRISPS

All you need is three ingredients to make these easy savoury snacks.

Serves 4
PREP TIME 20 minutes
COOK TIME 1 hour 30 minutes

Ingredients
500g baby courgettes
1 tablespoon sunflower oil
25g vegetarian Italian hard cheese,
  very finely grated

SmartPoints
2 per serving

 See page 6

Method

1 Preheat the oven to 120°C, fan 100°C, gas mark 1. Trim the courgettes, then thinly slice them lengthways into long, thin strips – use a mandoline if you have one, or simply cut as thin as you're able to with a sharp knife.

2 Transfer the courgettes to a wire rack set over a large baking sheet, brushing them with the oil as you go. Line up the courgette strips side-by-side, so they are just touching.

3 Season to taste, then scatter over the grated cheese. Bake for 1 hour 30 minutes until the courgettes are crisp and golden, then serve.

HOMEMADE CEREAL BARS

The tasty bakes are perfect for a mid-morning snack on the go.

Makes 18
PREP TIME 15 minutes
COOK TIME 25 minutes

Ingredients
250g rolled porridge oats
3 tablespoons coconut oil
150g ripe banana flesh (about
  1 large banana)
3 tablespoons clear honey
1½ teaspoons ground cinnamon
50g whole almonds
  roughly chopped
50g dried apricots, diced

4 SmartPoints
SmartPoints value   4 per bar   V

Method

1 Preheat the oven to 180°C, fan 160°C, gas mark 4
  and line a 22cm square cake tin with baking paper.

2 Put 50g of the oats into a food processor or blender with
  the coconut oil, banana and honey, then blend to a smooth
  mixture. Transfer to a bowl, then stir in the cinnamon, the
  remaining oats, the almonds and apricots.

3 Press the mixture into the prepared tin and smooth the top.
  Bake for 20-25 minutes until golden and firm on top. Leave
  in the tin to cool, then turn out onto a board and peel off
  the baking paper. Cut into 18 bars. The bars can be stored
  in an airtight container for 3-4 days, or you can individually
  wrap them in cling film and freeze them for up to 1 month
  – let them thaw for an hour or two before eating.

BLACKBERRY CLAFOUTIS

Our version of the classic French dessert includes fresh, juicy blackberries.

Serves 4
PREP TIME 15 minutes
COOK TIME 35 minutes

Ingredients
50g plain flour
1 teaspoon bicarbonate of soda
3 large eggs
1 teaspoon vanilla extract
½ teaspoon almond extract
200ml unsweetened almond milk
25g caster sugar
1 teaspoon rapeseed oil
200g sweet blackberries
1 tablespoon flaked almonds
1 teaspoon icing sugar

 SmartPoints
5 per serving **V**

Method

1 Preheat the oven to 180°C, fan 160°C, gas mark 4. Combine the flour and bicarbonate of soda in a mixing bowl. Whisk in the eggs, one at a time, until you have a smooth batter, then whisk in the vanilla extract, almond extract and almond milk. Stir in the sugar and set aside.

2 Put a 20-22cm cast-iron frying pan or flameproof metal pie dish over a low heat to warm, then remove from the heat and rub quickly with the oil. Pour in the batter, scatter over the berries and top with the flaked almonds.

3 Bake for 30-35 minutes until puffed and golden. Dust with the icing sugar to serve.

Desserts

CARAMELISED PINEAPPLE & RUM SLICES

Bring a taste of the tropics to your table with this wonderfully simple dessert.

Serves 6
PREP TIME 15 minutes,
plus marinating
COOK TIME 20 minutes

Ingredients
3 tablespoons dark rum
3 tablespoons agave syrup
1 tablespoon low-fat spread
1 small pineapple, halved
lengthways

For the yogurt
300g 0% fat vanilla yogurt
300g 0% fat natural Greek yogurt
Grated zest of 2 limes and juice of 1

 SmartPoints
3 per serving

   See page 6

Method

1 Preheat the oven to 220°C, fan 200°C, gas mark 7. Put the rum, agave syrup and low-fat spread in a small pan and set over a medium heat. Bring to the boil and simmer for 2 minutes.

2 Cut each pineapple half into 3 chunky wedges, then cut away the woody core from each wedge. Put each wedge skin-side down on a chopping board and make criss-cross cuts into the flesh, then transfer to a roasting tin. Brush the syrup over the cut sides of the pineapple wedges – you can leave to marinate in the fridge for up to 24 hours, if you have time.

3 Roast the pineapple for 15 minutes until golden. Meanwhile fold together the vanilla yogurt, Greek yogurt, lime juice and zest in a small bowl.

4 Serve the pineapple warm with the lime yogurt.

MINI CHEESECAKES

This trio of small but indulgent puds is perfect for parties.

Makes 12
PREP TIME 30 minutes, plus chilling
COOK TIME 5 minutes

Ingredients
6 ginger nut biscuits
1 tablespoon coconut oil
200g low-fat soft cheese
250g quark

For the raspberry ripple
50g raspberries, plus 4 extra
  berries to decorate
4 teaspoons icing sugar
¼ teaspoons vanilla extract
Grated zest of ½ lemon

For the zesty lime
½ x 23g pack sugar-free lime
  jelly crystals
Grated zest of 1 lime and the
  juice of ½

For the white chocolate
50g white chocolate, broken
  into chunks
½ teaspoon vanilla paste

Method

1 Put the ginger nuts and coconut oil in a food processor and whizz to crumbs. Divide between 12 small glasses, then press down to make a firm base. Chill the bases while you make the cheesecake fillings.

2 In a mixing bowl, beat together the soft cheese and quark until smooth, then divide the mixture equally between 3 smaller bowls.

3 For the raspberry ripple cheesecake, crush the 50g raspberries lightly with a fork. Mix ⅓ of the crushed raspberries into one of the soft cheese portions, along with the icing sugar, vanilla and lemon zest, then swirl the rest of the crushed raspberries through the mixture and divide between 4 of the glasses. Top each with a whole raspberry.

4 For the zesty lime cheesecakes, put the jelly crystals into a heatproof jug and stir in 150ml boiling water until the crystals have dissolved. Leave to cool, then whisk 100ml of the jelly into the second cream cheese portion, along with the lime zest and juice. Divide the mixture between 4 of the glasses and chill for 1 hour until firm, then pour the remaining jelly over the top of the cheesecake filling.

5 For for the white chocolate cheesecakes, reserve 10g of the chocolate. Put the rest in a heatproof bowl set over a small pan of simmering water, stirring occasionally until the chocolate has melted. Remove from the heat and stir in the vanilla paste and the remaining cream cheese portion. Divide the mixture between the remaining 4 glasses and grate over the reserved chocolate.

6 Put all the glasses on a small tray and chill for at least 2 hours to set, then serve.

RASPBERRY RIPPLE

SmartPoints
3 per cheesecake

ZESTY LIME

SmartPoints
2 per cheesecake

WHITE CHOCOLATE

SmartPoints
6 per cheesecake

Desserts

MANGO & COCONUT BRULEE

Juicy mango slices and coconut yogurt are topped with caramelised coconut.

Serves 4
PREP TIME 10 minutes
COOK TIME 5 minutes

Ingredients
3 ripe mangoes, peeled
Juice of 1 orange
2 tablespoons demerara sugar
1 tablespoon desiccated coconut
200g dairy-free coconut yogurt

SmartPoints
4 per serving

  See page 6

Method

1 Stand each mango on its end and cut down either side of the stone as close as you can so you have thick slices. Cut each slice into chunky wedges and put in a large baking dish. Drizzle the orange juice over the mango.

2 Preheat the grill to high. Crush the sugar with the coconut using a pestle and mortar or mini food processor.

3 Spoon the yogurt over the mango, then scatter the sugar and coconut mixture over the yogurt. Grill for 3-5 minutes until the sugar melts and caramelises. Serve warm, or chill in the fridge and serve cold.

RASPBERRY & ELDERFLOWER SORBET

Cool, fresh and fruity, this dessert features some favourite summer flavours.

Serves 6
PREP TIME 15 minutes,
plus freezing
COOK TIME 5 minutes

Ingredients
500g raspberries, plus extra to serve
4 tablespoons elderflower cordial
50g caster or granulated sugar
3 large egg whites*
Fresh mixed berries, to serve

 **SmartPoints**
2 per serving

  See page 6

Method

1 Whizz the raspberries in a blender or food processor to a smooth purée, then press through a sieve into a bowl and discard the seeds.

2 Put the elderflower cordial and sugar in a small pan with 4 tablespoons water. Stir over a very low heat until the sugar has dissolved, then increase the heat, bring to a boil and let the mixture bubble vigorously for 2 minutes. Remove from the heat and stir in the raspberry purée, then set aside to cool.

3 Beat the egg whites in a clean bowl until stiff peaks form. Fold ⅓ of the egg white into the raspberry mixture until combined. Then, with a large metal spoon or spatula, gently fold the rest of the egg whites through the raspberry mixture. Be as gentle as you can – you want the mixture to be well combined, but still light and airy. Transfer the mixture into a plastic container or loaf tin, then cover with clingfilm and freeze overnight.

4 Take the sorbet out of the freezer 15 minutes before serving. Scoop into bowls and serve with fresh berries.

*Contains raw egg white.

BAKED APPLES WITH OATY CRUMB TOPPING

This warming pud is the perfect ending to dinner on a chilly evening.

Serves 4
PREP TIME 20 minutes
COOK TIME 40 minutes

Ingredients
4 Braeburn apples, or any other
  eating apples
150ml pomegranate juice
50g rolled oats
25g plain flour
1 teaspoon ground cinnamon
25g low-fat spread
2 teaspoons tahini
1 tablespoon demerara sugar
2 teaspoons sesame seeds
120g 0% fat natural Greek yogurt

 **SmartPoints**
6 per serving

Method

1 Preheat the oven to 180°C, fan 160°C, gas mark 4. Core the apples, then cut them in half through the middle – not top to bottom. Pour the pomegranate juice into a baking dish and add 100ml water. Arrange the apples, cut-side down, in the dish, then cover the dish with foil and bake for 20 minutes.

2 Meanwhile, combine the oats, flour and cinnamon in a bowl. Using your fingertips, rub the low-fat spread and tahini into the dry ingredients until the mixture clumps together in large crumbs. Stir through the sugar and sesame seeds.

3 Remove the baking dish from the oven and discard the foil. Carefully turn over the apples so they sit cut-side-up. Sprinkle the crumble mixture evenly over each apple half, then return to the oven for 15-20 minutes until the crumble is golden and the apples are soft. Serve warm with the Greek yogurt.

Desserts

PEACH & PROSECCO JELLY

A simple, elegant dessert perfect for serving to dinner guests.

Makes 4
PREP TIME 10 minutes, plus chilling
COOK TIME 5 minutes

Ingredients
5 sheets leaf gelatine
250ml pink Prosecco
1 tablespoon lemon juice
1 tablespoon caster sugar
250ml sugar-free lemonade
3 ripe peaches (use a mixture of yellow and white flesh ones if you can), halved and stone removed

 SmartPoints
3 per jelly

 See page 6

Method

1 Put the gelatine sheets in a shallow dish, cover with cold water and leave for 5 minutes to soften.

2 Put 150ml Prosecco, the lemon juice and sugar in a small pan and heat gently until the sugar has dissolved and the liquid is almost boiling. Remove from the heat.

3 Remove the softened gelatine sheets from the water and squeeze out any excess liquid, then whisk them into the hot Prosecco mixture until dissolved, stir in the remaining Prosecco and the lemonade.

4 Dice the peach halves and divide between 4 glasses or serving bowls. Pour over the Prosecco mixture and chill for at least 4 hours until the jelly has set. The jellies will keep for up to 3 days in the fridge though, so you can make them ahead of time.

Drinks

STRAWBERRY & BUTTERMILK SMOOTHIE

Whizz up one of these in minutes for a quick and tasty breakfast drink.

Makes 2
PREP TIME 5 minutes

Ingredients
**200g ripe strawberries, plus extra
  strawberries to serve**
75g ripe banana flesh
150ml buttermilk
½ teaspoon vanilla extract

 SmartPoints
5 per serving

 See page 6

Method
1 Put all the ingredients in a blender with 100ml cold water and whizz until smooth. If you like, you can add a few ice cubes then whizz for a few more seconds to thin out the smoothie and chill it.

2 Divide the smoothie between two glasses, top with the extra strawberries and serve.

MAKE IT TROPICAL
Instead of the strawberries, use 200g ripe mango flesh and serve topped with a few mango chunks for an extra **2 SmartPoints**.

Drinks

CHOCOLATE CHAI

For a warming drink on wintry evenings, this spiced hot chocolate is ideal.

Serves 4
PREP TIME 5 minutes
COOK TIME 10 minutes

Ingredients
50g low-calorie hot chocolate
  powder
2 tablespoons cocoa powder
1 teaspoon ground ginger
1 litre skimmed milk
6 cardamom pods
1 large cinnamon stick, plus 4 small
  cinnamon sticks to serve (optional)
4 black peppercorns

SmartPoints
6 per serving

 See page 6

Method

1 In a small bowl, mix together the hot chocolate powder, cocoa and ginger, then add just enough milk to form a smooth paste. Once the paste is smooth, stir in enough milk to reach a pouring consistency.

2 Use the side of a knife to crush the cardamom pods open, then snap the cinnamon stick into a few pieces. Put into a pan with the peppercorns, the chocolate mixture and the rest of the milk.

3 Put the pan over a very low heat and warm slowly until the milk is steaming, but not boiling or bubbling. Strain into mugs and serve with the small cinnamon sticks (if using).

MAKE IT A MORNING PICK-ME-UP
For a more authentic version of chai, add a teabag to the mixture while you heat the milk.

BLACKBERRY & ROSEMARY FIZZ

Fresh berries and rosemary make this summery sparkler irresistible.

Serves 4
PREP TIME 10 minutes

Ingredients
75g blackberries, plus a few
  extra to serve
Juice of 1 lemon
4 small sprigs fresh rosemary
400ml diet lemonade

 SmartPoints
1 per serving

  See page 6

Method

1 Put the blackberries and lemon juice in a small food processor or blender and whizz to a smooth purée. Press through a sieve or tea strainer into a small bowl and discard the seeds.

2 Divide the blackberry purée between 4 Champagne flutes or cocktail glasses. Put the rosemary sprigs on a chopping board and use a rolling pin to lightly roll over the sprigs and crush the leaves a little. Add a sprig to each glass with a few ice cubes.

3 Top up the glasses with the lemonade, stir everything together using the rosemary sprigs and serve.

MAKE IT A CELEBRATION
Instead of lemonade, top up with 400ml Prosecco for a total of **3 SmartPoints** per drink.

MAKE IT A TALL SPRITZER FOR 2
Divide the blackberry purée between 2 tall glasses, add the rosemary and ice, then stir 100ml white wine into each glass and top up with 150ml sugar-free lemonade for a total of **4 SmartPoints** per drink.

Drinks

PINEAPPLE, LIME & COCONUT COOLER

Fresh and zingy, this is a great way to cool down on a hot summer's day.

Serves 4
PREP TIME 10 minutes

Ingredients
800ml chilled coconut water
125g ripe pineapple chunks
4 teaspoons agave syrup
Juice of 3 limes, plus lime slices,
   to serve
Handful fresh mint leaves, to serve

SmartPoints
4 per serving

 See page 6

Method

1 Put ⅓ of the coconut water in a blender with the pineapple chunks, agave syrup and lime juice, then blend until smooth.

2 Pour the pineapple mixture into a large jug and stir in the remaining coconut water. Add the lime slices, ice cubes and mint leaves and mix again. Serve immediately.

MAKE IT GREEN

Instead of pineapple, try making this with 125g peeled kiwi fruit for no additional SmartPoints.

Meal plans

5 SIMPLE & SPEEDY DAILY MENUS

Day	Breakfast	Lunch
1	Porridge made with 30g oats and 150ml skimmed milk, topped with fresh blueberries and 1 teaspoon cinnamon 5 SmartPoints	Tuna lentil Niçoise, p70 2 SmartPoints
2	1 slice toasted Weight Watchers Soft White Danish Bread topped with 30g ricotta cheese and 100g halved cherry tomatoes 3 SmartPoints	Squash & spinach frittata, p41 2 SmartPoints
3	2 shredded wheat with 150ml skimmed milk and 1 sliced banana 6 SmartPoints	Toasted chicken sandwich, p90 4 SmartPoints
4	2 soft-boiled eggs with 2 slices toasted Weight Watchers Malted Danish Bread and 1 teaspoon low-fat spread 4 SmartPoints	Pea, mint & ham soup, p118, with 1 toasted herby pitta, p166 6 SmartPoints
5	3 scrambled eggs with 60g smoked salmon and 1 toasted bagel thin 6 SmartPoints	Chickpea & goat's cheese salad, p148 6 SmartPoints

Busy days require quick and easy meal solutions. Planning ahead helps you save time, as do these suggestions for five days' worth of fuss-free meals.

Dinner	Dessert/snack	Total SmartPoints
Sticky peanut butter chicken, p98 — 9 SmartPoints	Homemade cereal bars, p182 — 4 SmartPoints	20 SmartPoints
Classic beef burger, p124, with tomato & red onion salad, p138 — 11 SmartPoints	Peach & Prosecco jelly, p196 (make ahead) — 3 SmartPoints	19 SmartPoints
Pea pesto pasta, p156 — 7 SmartPoints	Greek salad skewers, p174 — 2 SmartPoints	19 SmartPoints
Chicken Caprese, p84 — 7 SmartPoints	Mango & coconut brûlée, p190 — 4 SmartPoints	21 SmartPoints
Honey roast salmon, p74 with potato salad (make ahead), p80 — 8 SmartPoints	Raspberry & elderflower sorbet (make ahead), p192 — 2 SmartPoints	22 SmartPoints

5 DAILY VEGETARIAN MENUS

Day	Breakfast	Lunch
1	2 slices Weight Watchers Thick Wholemeal Bread topped with 2 poached eggs and spinach leaves 4 SmartPoints	Roasted squash & freekeh salad, p162 10 SmartPoints
2	Eggs Benedict, p28 4 SmartPoints	Goat's cheese & asparagus frittata, p42 4 SmartPoints
3	Porridge made with 30g oats and 150ml skimmed milk, topped with a sliced banana 5 SmartPoints	Chickpea & tomato soup, p148 0 SmartPoints
4	Blackberries, strawberries and blueberries with 0% fat natural Greek yogurt 0 SmartPoints	Greek orzo salad, p144 10 SmartPoints
5	Homemade cereal bar, p182 4 SmartPoints	Roasted tomato crustless quiche, p32 2 SmartPoints

Even if you're not a vegetarian, having the occasional meat-free day can keep things interesting. Here are five suggestions for daily veggie menus.

Dinner	Dessert/snack	Total SmartPoints
Quorn, cauliflower & spinach curry with mini naan bread, p150 — 5 SmartPoints	Mango & coconut brûlée, p190 — 4 SmartPoints	23 SmartPoints
Creamy mushroom pasta, p159 — 7 SmartPoints	Caramelised pineapple & rum slices, p186 — 3 SmartPoints	18 SmartPoints
Spring vegetable risotto, p154 — 8 SmartPoints	Baked apples with oaty crumb topping, p194 — 6 SmartPoints	19 SmartPoints
Halloumi burger with caramelised onions, p142 — 8 SmartPoints	Raspberry & elderflower sorbet, p192 — 2 SmartPoints	20 SmartPoints
Mediterranean vegetable pasta bake, p160 — 10 SmartPoints	Toasted herby pittas, p166 with Tzatziki, p34 — 4 SmartPoints	20 SmartPoints

5 DAILY FAMILY MENUS

Day	Breakfast		Lunch
1	1 toasted crumpet topped with 100g baked beans and 2 lean bacon medallions per person 8 SmartPoints		Chicken enchiladas, p88 7 SmartPoints
2	25g no added sugar puffed wheat with 150ml skimmed milk and fresh berries 4 SmartPoints		Chorizo & feta frittata, p42 3 SmartPoints
3	0% fat natural Greek yogurt with fresh fruit 0 SmartPoints		Roasted tomato & basil pasta, p157 7 SmartPoints
4	Porridge made with 30g oats and 150ml skimmed milk, topped with fresh blueberries and 1 teaspoon cinnamon 5 SmartPoints		Salmon pittas, p62 5 SmartPoints
5	Scrambled eggs and sliced tomatoes in a warmed tortilla wrap 4 SmartPoints		Chicken with pesto pasta, p90 8 SmartPoints

Keeping all the family happy with nutritious, tasty food, while staying on track yourself can be tricky. These menu suggestions mean everyone can enjoy the same meals and you can add sides and extras for other family members.

Dinner	Dessert/snack	Total SmartPoints
Turkey & mushroom lasagne, p96 3 SmartPoints	Veggie scotch eggs, p172 4 SmartPoints	22 SmartPoints
Coconut-crusted fish fingers, p56 12 SmartPoints	Crispy bean fries with tomato dipping sauce, p176 3 SmartPoints	22 SmartPoints
Chickpea Bolognese, p158 9 SmartPoints	Baked apples with oaty crumb topping, p194 6 SmartPoints	22 SmartPoints
Classic beef burger, p124 8 SmartPoints	Homemade cereal bars, p182 4 SmartPoints	22 SmartPoints
Sausage & sweet potato bake, p120 6 SmartPoints	Blackberry clafoutis, p184 5 SmartPoints	23 SmartPoints

5 DAILY NO COUNT MENUS

Day	Breakfast		Lunch
1	1 toasted crumpet topped with sliced banana		Pea, mint & ham soup, p118, with 1 slice calorie controlled brown bread
2	Porridge made with 30g oats and 150ml skimmed milk, topped with fresh raspberries and 0% fat natural Greek yogurt		Toasted chicken sandwich, p90
3	Porridge made with 30g oats and 150ml skimmed milk, topped with a sliced banana		Salmon, pea & lemon frittata, p43, with spicy chilli chips, p79
4	3 scrambled eggs and 6 grilled button mushrooms on 1 toasted sandwich thin		Chickpea & tomato soup, p148, served with a warmed Weight Watchers Wholemeal Pitta Bread
5	2 bacon medallions, lettuce and tomato in a warmed Weight Watchers White Wrap		Squash & spinach frittata, p41

If you're following No Count, try these easy daily menus with ideas for breakfast, lunch and dinner, plus a dessert or snack.

Dinner	Dessert/snack
Mexican style chicken, p103, with herby brown rice, p51	30g plain popcorn (no added oil or flavours)
Quorn, cauliflower & spinach curry, p150, with Pea & coriander rice, p110	Spiced roast chickpeas, p148
Rosemary & thyme sandwich burger, p126, with spicy chilli chips, p79	Fresh fruit salad with 0% fat natural Greek yogurt
Butternut squash & chilli pasta, p158	Tzatziki, p34 with vegetable crudités
Cod & chickpea curry, p66, with herby brown rice, p51	Sugar-free jelly with tinned or fresh fruit

5 DAILY MENUS TO SUIT YOU

Day	Breakfast	Lunch
COOKING FOR 1	2 slices Weight Watchers Malted Danish Bread topped with ½ avocado, freshly ground black pepper and chilli flakes 6 SmartPoints	Ham & Waldorf tartine, p118 5 SmartPoints
JUST THE 2 OF US	Scrambled eggs and sliced tomatoes in a warmed tortilla wrap 4 SmartPoints	Toasted chicken sandwiches, p90 4 SmartPoints
SUMMER EATING	Chunks of fresh melon, pineapple, kiwi and strawberries with 0% fat natural Greek yogurt 0 SmartPoints	Prawn, broccoli & rice noodle salad, p73 8 SmartPoints
WINTERY DAY	Porridge made with 30g oats and 150ml skimmed milk, topped with 1 chopped apple stewed in 1 teaspoon cinnamon and 1 teaspoon brown sugar 6 SmartPoints	Pea, mint & ham soup, p118 2 SmartPoints
BUSY DAY ON THE GO	Homemade cereal bar, p182 (make ahead) 4 SmartPoints	Chicken & grape salad, p90 4 SmartPoints

Not every day's the same – your meal choices might be influenced by who you're with, the weather outside or even how busy you are. Try these one-off menu ideas…

Dinner	Dessert/snack	Total SmartPoints
Mediterranean omelette with smoked salmon, p48 5 SmartPoints	Homemade cereal bar, p182 4 SmartPoints	20 SmartPoints
Prawn katsu burgers, p60 10 SmartPoints	Strawberry & buttermilk smoothie, p198 5 SmartPoints	23 SmartPoints
Chilli beef with houmous, p114 10 SmartPoints	Raspberry & elderflower sorbet, p192 2 SmartPoints	20 SmartPoints
Beef & mushroom stew, p116 8 SmartPoints	Baked apples with oaty crumb topping, p194 6 SmartPoints	22 SmartPoints
Celeriac-topped fish pie, p58 (make ahead & freeze) 7 SmartPoints	Veggie scotch eggs, p172 (make ahead) 4 SmartPoints	19 SmartPoints

5 GLUTEN-FREE DAILY MENUS

Day	Breakfast		Lunch
1	Chunks of fresh melon, pineapple, kiwi and strawberries with 0% fat natural Greek yogurt 0 SmartPoints		Tuna lentil Niçoise, p70 2 SmartPoints
2	Mexican-style scrambled eggs, p30 3 SmartPoints		Ham & leek risotto, p118 8 SmartPoints
3	Porridge made with 30g oats and 150ml skimmed milk, topped with a sliced banana 5 SmartPoints		Goat's cheese & asparagus frittata, p42 4 SmartPoints
4	A smoothie made from 25g porridge oats, 1 banana and 150ml skimmed milk, blended 5 SmartPoints		Potato, spinach & chicken salad, p90 5 SmartPoints
5	2 bacon medallions, 3 tablespoons baked beans, 1 poached egg, 1 grilled tomato, 6 grilled button mushrooms, 1 slice gluten-free bread and 1 teaspoon low-fat spread 8 SmartPoints		Roasted tomato crustless quiche, p32 2 SmartPoints

Being gluten-free is not always easy, as wheat-based ingredients are present in so many foods. These daily menus provide all the taste and nutrition you need, without any of the gluten (see page 6).

Dinner	Dessert/snack	Total SmartPoints
Stir-fried beef with mango, p128, with coconut rice, p138 13 SmartPoints	Courgette & cheese crisps, p180 2 SmartPoints Peach & Prosecco jelly, p196 3 SmartPoints	20 SmartPoints
Chicken Caprese, p84, with hasselback potatoes, p109 9 SmartPoints	Caramelised pineapple & rum slices, p186 3 SmartPoints	23 SmartPoints
Honey roast salmon, p74, with potato salad, p80 8 SmartPoints	Raspberry & elderflower sorbet, p192 2 SmartPoints	19 SmartPoints
Roast pork with noodle salad, p134 7 SmartPoints	Crispy green bean fries, p176 3 SmartPoints	20 SmartPoints
Marmalade chicken, p101 6 SmartPoints	Mango & coconut brûlée, p190 4 SmartPoints	20 SmartPoints

5 MENUS FOR SPECIAL OCCASIONS

Day	Starter	Main
EASY BUT IMPRESSIVE DINNER PARTY	Crispy green bean 'fries' with tomato dipping sauce, p176 — 3 SmartPoints	Chicken Caprese, p84 — 7 SmartPoints
FAMILY SUNDAY LUNCH	Chickpea & tomato soup, p148 — 0 SmartPoints	Marmalade chicken traybake, p101 — 6 SmartPoints
SPECIAL CELEBRATION	Mini sweetcorn & feta fritters, p178 — 2 SmartPoints	Sea bass fillets with chorizo crumb, p64 — 5 SmartPoints
FEEDING A CROWD	Cheese fondue with veggie dippers, p46 — 3 SmartPoints	Pork, apple & white bean stew, p130 — 5 SmartPoints
NO-COOK LUNCH	Toasted herby pittas, p166, with Beetroot dip, p34 — 4 SmartPoints	Chicken & grape salad, p90 — 4 SmartPoints

Entertaining guests? Here are 5 delicious menus with starters, main courses, side dishes and desserts to suit almost any occasion.

Side	Dessert	Total SmartPoints
Spinach & pine nut salad, p52 3 SmartPoints	Peach & Prosecco jelly, p196 3 SmartPoints	16 SmartPoints
Mini hasselback potatoes, p109 5 SmartPoints	Blackberry clafoutis, p184 5 SmartPoints	16 SmartPoints
Potato salad, p80 4 SmartPoints	Caramelised pineapple & rum slices, p186 3 SmartPoints	14 SmartPoints
Celeriac, potato & parsnip mash, p137 4 SmartPoints	Cheesecake shots, p188 2-6 SmartPoints	14-18 SmartPoints
Skinny coleslaw, p52 0 SmartPoints	Raspberry & elderflower sorbet, p192 2 SmartPoints	10 SmartPoints

RECIPE INDEX

RECIPE INDEX

NO COUNT INDEX

SMARTPOINTS INDEX